DEATH

Living Faiths

DEATH

Edited by John Prickett

LUTTERWORTH EDUCATIONAL

GUILDFORD & LONDON

First published 1980

ISBN 0 7188 2443 1

Photoset, printed and bound
in Great Britain by
REDWOOD BURN LIMITED
Trowbridge & Esher

CONTENTS

ACKNOWLEDGEMENTS

The editor and publishers are grateful to all those who have given their permission to reproduce extracts from their orders of service, including the following owners of copyrighted material:

Baha'i Publishing Trust for extracts from *Baha'i Prayers for Special Occasions*.
National Liturgical Commission of England and Wales for extracts from *The Funeral Rite* (1971).
Antiochan Orthodox Christian Archdiocese of New York and all North America, for extracts from the *Service Book of the Holy Orthodox-Catholic Apostolic Church* (5th edition) compiled by I.S. Hapgood.
The Reform Synagogues of Great Britain for extracts from *Forms of Prayer for Jewish Worship*.
George Allen & Unwin (Publishers) Ltd., for extracts from *Sacred Writings of the Sikhs* by Trilochan Singh.

LIST OF CONTRIBUTORS

The editor wishes gratefully to acknowledge his debt to the following who have contributed to the sections on the different faiths, although he takes full responsibility for the final form of each extract.

Baha'i Faith	Mr. Philip Hainsworth
Buddhism	The Ven. Dr. Vajiragnana The Rev. Jack Austin
Christianity	Monsignor K. Nichols The Rev. K. Ottosson
Hinduism	Pandit V. Narayan Professor S.N. Bharadwaj
Humanism	Mr. Harold Blackham
Islam	Mr. R. El Droubie
Judaism	Mr. Paul Shaw
Sikhism	Dr. Trilochan Singh

FURTHER INFORMATION

The following is a list of addresses which may be useful to teachers who wish to obtain information beyond the scope of this book.

Baha'i Faith

National Spiritual Assembly of
   the Baha'is of the UK
27 Rutland Gate
London SW7 1PD
Tel 01-584 2566

Buddhism

Buddhist Society
58 Eccleston Square
London SW1
Tel 01-834 5858

Christianity

Friends Community
   Relations Committee
Friends House
Euston Road
London NW1 2BJ
Tel 01-387 3601

Community & Race Relations
   Unit
British Council of Churches
2 Eaton Gate
London SW1 9BT
Tel 01-730 9611

Church Missionary Society
157 Waterloo Road
London SE1 8UU
Tel 01-928 8681

National Society
Church House
Dean's Yard
Westminster SW1
Tel 01-222 9011

Division of Social
   Responsibility of the
   Methodist Church
1 Central Buildings
Matthew Parker Street
London SW1H 9NH
Tel 01-222 8589

Westminster Religious Education Centre
23 Kensington Square
London W8 5HN
Tel 01–937 7470

Missions and Other Faiths
   Committee
United Reformed Church
86 Tavistock Place
London WC1H 9RT
Tel 01–837 7661

Hinduism

Raja Yoga Centre (Ishvarya
   Vishwa-Vidyalaya)
98 Tennyson Road
London NW6
Tel 01–328 2478

Ramakrishna Vedanta Centre
Unity House
Blind Lane
Bourne End
Bucks SL8 5LG

Vedic Mission (Arya Samaj)
    London
4 Horsenden Avenue
Sudbury Hill
Greenford
Middlesex

Humanism

British Humanist Association
13 Prince of Wales Terrace
London W8 5PG
Tel 01–937 2341

Islam

Islamic Foundation
223 London Road
Leicester LE2 1ZE
Tel 0533–700725

Islamic Cultural Centre
146 Park Road
London NW8 7RG
Tel 01–724 3363–7

Muslim Educational Trust
55 Portland Road
Birmingham 16
Contact: Dr. A.M. Rajput
Tel 021-454 0671

Muslim Educational Trust
130 Stroud Green
London N4 3RZ
Tel 01–272 8502

Judaism

The Education Officer
Central Jewish Lecture Com-
    mittee of the Board of Depu-
    ties of British Jews
Fourth Floor
Woburn House
Upper Woburn Place
London WC1H 0EP
Tel 01–387 3952

Jewish Education Bureau
8 Westcombe Avenue
Leeds LS8 2BS
Tel 0532–663613

Council of Christians and Jews
48 Onslow Gardens
London SW7 3PX
Tel 01–589 8854

Sikhism

Sikh Cultural Society of Great
    Britain
88 Mollison Way
Edgware
Middlesex
Tel 01–952 1215

Supreme Council of the Sikhs
    UK
162 Great West Road
Hounslow, Middlesex
President: Mr. J.S. Sandhu
Tel 01–570 4424
Secretary: Mr. A.S. Samra
Tel 01–570 4424

Miscellaneous

R.E. Centre
West London Institute of
  Higher Education
Lancaster House
Borough Road
Isleworth
Middlesex TW7 5DU
Tel 01–560 5991

R.E. Centre
Westhill College of Education
Selly Oak
Birmingham B29 6LL
Tel 021–472 1563

The Christian Muslim Centre
Selly Oak Colleges
Birmingham B29 6LE
Tel 021–472 4231

York R.E. Centre
College of Ripon and York St.
  John
Lord Mayor's Walk
York YO3 7EX
Tel 0904–56771

R.E. Centre
Homerton College
Cambridge CB2 2PH
Tel 0223–44122

University of Lancaster
Project on Religious Education
Cartmel College
Bailrigg
Lancaster
Tel Lancaster 65202

Standing Conference on Inter-
  Faith Dialogue in Education
C/o World Congress of Faiths
28 Powis Gardens
London W11 1JG
Tel 01–727 2607

Information and Advisory
  Officer
SHAP Working Party on
  World Religions in Edu-
  cation
Borough Road College
Isleworth
Middlesex TW7 5DU
Tel 01–560 5991

North West Regional Inter-
  Faith Conference
Edge Hill College of Higher
  Education
St. Helens Road
Ormskirk
Lancashire L39 4QP

FOREWORD

In this second book of the Living Faiths series our educational approach is identical with that described in the Foreword to the first. We there referred to a report of a working party of the Religious Education Council which described their view of religious education in the following terms:

> In the present situation we see religious education in schools as helping pupils to be informed and concerned about religions and other life-stances rather than attaching them to any particular faith.

An appendix to that same report stated that

> much of the material now being produced by believing bodies either assumes that the pupils accept the beliefs described or that the purpose of education is to persuade them to do so. If faith systems could produce authentic information about themselves which, while doing full justice to the depth of their own conviction, assumed an uncommitted spirit of enquiry in the students, the teacher's task, as we have envisaged it, would be generally assisted.

The books in this series are an attempt to produce such authentic information for the use of teachers and students of world faiths. In this book, following the introductory essays by Professor Parrinder and Dr. Brian Gates, we have endeavoured, within the inevitable limitations of space, to present a brief account of attitudes to death (and what may lie beyond it) in each faith. We have also given, where appropriate, extracts from funeral liturgies and some account of burial ceremonies.

These accounts, given by adherents of each faith represented, are inevitably uneven but that unevenness itself may reflect something of the different approach to the subject in the various faiths and no attempt has been made to iron it out.

In our first book, *Initiation Rites*, the Christian section in-

I

cluded extracts from the initiation rites of the principal Christian denominations. This we felt to be justified by the fact that there were significant differences in these rites and because the book would be used mainly in Britain and North America.

In considering attitudes to death, however, we felt that the most significant differences within Christianity were between the Roman Catholics, the Protestants and the Eastern Orthodox. We have therefore confined the Christian section to these three. This makes for a better balance in the book as a whole since the Christian section is not as predominant as it would otherwise have been.

Most of these papers were originally presented to the Annual Conference of the Standing Conference on Inter-Faith Dialogue in Education held in Bedford in 1977. A few have been written subsequently. The liturgical extracts have, for the most part, been chosen by the editor after consultation with the contributors. This selection often raises controversial issues concerning different versions, especially where translation is involved. The editor accepts full responsibility for the final choices recognising that in such a matter it is not possible to please everyone. When the choice has been between a traditional form and a recent revision, the most recent version has usually been chosen.

The editor wishes to express his thanks to the contributors, whose names are listed elsewhere, and to Rabbi Hugo Gryn (Chairman of the Standing Conference) who has very kindly read the book in manuscript form. We are also indebted to the Noel Buxton Trust which has helped us financially with the preparation of this book.

John Prickett

PART I
DEATH IN THE
WORLD FAITHS

Introduction
by Geoffrey Parrinder

Birth and death are the two events which come to every human
being and all religions are concerned with them. 'Rites of
passage' are performed on both occasions; these are ceremonies
in which the person passes from one stage to another and is
guided on his way.

Belief in the survival of death is found in all religions and it is
perhaps mankind's oldest religious conviction. Far back in pre-
history traces remain of such an idea, in the way in which
bodies were buried and in which tools and ornaments were laid
beside them for use in the life to come.

In historical religions there is great variety of teaching about
death and its consequences, from the resurrection taught by
monotheistic religions to the reincarnation held by religions of
India and beyond. Serious reasons are given for these beliefs
and they arise from the general doctrines of the religion in
question. It might be thought that belief in the survival of death
arose from wishful thinking, from the reluctance of men to
accept that their lives came to an end at death. But attention
must be given to the wider pattern of belief, and all that it
implies about the natures of God and man.

For convenience living religions may be roughly divided into
prophetic and wisdom religions, but this division is only
approximate, for prophecy and wisdom may appear in both
areas. However, it is better to make such a division than to

speak of western and eastern, or monotheistic and pantheistic, for that would cause even more confusion and overlapping. The prophetic religions indicated here are the Jewish, Islamic and Christian religions, and the wisdom religions are the Hindu, Buddhist and far-eastern faiths, with smaller traditions in both areas.

1. Prophetic Religions

a) Judaism

Judaism is the term used here in the broad sense which includes the early religion of the Hebrews, as well as the later biblical and post-biblical developments. It is often said that early Hebrew religion was this-worldly, concerned only with life on earth, and it is true that belief in a resurrection did not appear until a late biblical stage. However, there are plenty of traces in the early parts of the Bible which show that the ancient Israelites shared beliefs in the survival of death with neighbouring nations.

Graves, especially those of important people, were not only burying-places but often became, or were already, sanctuaries and places of pilgrimage. The grave of Sarah at the cave of Machpelah had an altar to the Lord, and the bones of Joseph were carried to Shechem which was or became a holy place. The same might be said of the graves of other famous people. It is not known what ceremonies were held at the graves, but they may have become assimilated to the worship of God.

Well-known phrases in the Bible speak of a man being 'gathered to his fathers', 'sleeping with his fathers', or being 'laid in the sepulchre with his fathers', and such phrases suggest, however vaguely, that a man joined his ancestors in the sleep of death.

In developing Hebrew religion there appeared the notion of Sheol, the abode of the departed. This is parallel to Babylonian belief in an immense city under the earth, enclosed by seven walls and gates, in total darkness, where the shades of men glided about in dark and sorrow. In the Bible Sheol is spoken of as 'the land of darkness' or 'the land of forgetfulness'. Job spoke of the 'bars of Sheol' and Hezekiah said, 'I shall go into the gates of Sheol' (Is. 38:10). In the rather dismal Psalm 88 we read, 'my life draws near unto Sheol . . . like the slain that lie in the grave, whom thou rememberest no more.' It seems that the psalmist imagined that God was not concerned with the departed shades and they did not remember him.

Later Jewish and Christian thought found such pessimism hard to swallow, and the favourite Psalm 23 which ends, 'I will dwell in the house of the Lord for length of days' was interpreted to mean 'for ever'. Similarly when the Book of Common Prayer was looking for a 'proper Psalm' for Easter Day it had to choose Psalm 16 which says, 'thou wilt not leave my soul to Sheol . . . in thy right hand there are pleasures for evermore,' though the original author may have thought, like Hezekiah, that he was being saved from death for a long life.

A most interesting Bible story is that of the dead prophet Samuel being evoked out of the earth by the medium of Endor (1 Sam. 28). This was clearly a spiritualistic seance and the woman (not a 'witch' but said to have 'a familiar spirit') cried out that she saw an old man coming up out of the ground, 'covered with a robe' like a prophet. Samuel, no doubt through the woman, spoke doom to Saul who in his happier days had tried to suppress such practices as the evocation of the dead.

While there are many hints of belief in the survival of death in the early Bible, it is true nevertheless that the emphasis was upon living a good and righteous life here on earth. But it seems, as in other religions, that the sufferings and inequalities of life encouraged men to look beyond death for justification. Psalm 73 which begins with trouble for the upright and envy of the prosperity of the wicked, ends with confidence that God will 'afterwards receive me to glory' and be my portion 'for ever'. In Isaiah 26, perhaps a late verse, we read that 'thy dead shall live, my dead bodies shall arise . . . and the earth shall cast forth her dead.'

Job's famous cry (19:25), 'I know that my redeemer liveth . . . and after my skin has been destroyed, with my flesh I shall see God,' is in a corrupt text and it is difficult to be sure of the meaning. But the most positive passage in the Old Testament speaks of resurrection, in the late book of Daniel (12), compiled after great national suffering. 'Many of those that sleep in the dust of the earth shall awake, some to everlasting life, and some to shame and everlasting contempt.'

In the inter-testamental period the belief in a brighter future after death gathered momentum, perhaps under the influence of the Persian Zoroastrians who held clear beliefs in heaven and hell, angels and judgement. The Jews were under the Persian empire from the sixth to the fourth century, and its influence continued in later times. There was a steady growth of belief among the people in a hopeful immortality, though it was denied by priestly Sadducees who debated with the Pharisees that 'there is no resurrection, neither angel nor spirit.' This scepticism seems to have disappeared with the decline of the priestly caste at the fall of the temple in 70AD. In the popular synagogues the teaching of the scribes and Pharisees was clearly in resurrection, and in the Eighteen Benedictions still used in the Jewish liturgy comes the phrase, 'Blessed art thou, O Lord, who quickens the dead.'

The Jewish historian Josephus said that some of the Pharisees held 'that the souls of the good alone go into another body', which would perhaps be a kind of reincarnation. But such an idea, though taught by some of the Greeks, such as Plato in the last chapter of his *Republic*, was foreign to most Jewish belief. The idea appeared possibly in one gospel passage (John 9:2), but it was not developed, and Jewish and Christian doctrine taught life after death in a state ordered by God. The Talmud gave great importance to the resurrection of the dead and discussed many questions related to it. The Thirteen Principles of the Faith formulated by Maimonides in the twelfth century incorporated in the orthodox Jewish Daily Prayer Book, end with the clause, 'I believe with perfect faith that there will be a resurrection of the dead at the time when it shall please the Creator.'

b) Islam

There is never any doubt in the religion of the followers of Muhammad about life after death. Early statements of belief declared faith in God, his angels, his books, his apostles, and the final resurrection. The doctrine of the Last Judgement has been reckoned as the second great tenet of the Qur'an, after the unity of God. Basically it is that after death men will be restored to life to appear before God, and assigned to Paradise or Hell according to their good or evil deeds.

6

Death is regarded in the Qur'an as a simple certainty which happens at a stated time, 'when their time comes they cannot put it off an hour, nor can they bring it on' (16:63); and again, 'everyone is subject to death, and it is on the day of resurrection that you will be paid your rewards in fuli' (3:182). It is believed that the souls of the departed are taken into the charge of the angel of death and held until the resurrection, though the interval seems to them only like one day. Prayers may be said for the departed, but only if they have died in the faith. Muhammad is said to have prayed for the dead Christian ruler of Ethiopia, but he was unable to pray for his own father who had died a pagan.

The climax of history which brings the present world order to an end is referred to in many ways in the Qur'an, with vivid descriptions of its signs, especially in the shorter chapters at the end of the Qur'an (in the traditional arrangement which puts the short chapters last). The Day of Resurrection is also the Day of Judgement, Distinction or Gathering, or simply the Last Day, Hour or Event. The Day comes suddenly, preceded by a thunderclap or a blast of a trumpet. Then there will be a cosmic upheaval, the mountains dissolve, the seas boil, the sun is darkened, the stars fall and the sky is rolled up. God appears on a throne, surrounded by angels, and all nations are assembled. The graves are opened and all human beings are restored to life. Taken literally, this belief explains the aversion expressed by Muslims to cremation.

The people of Mecca mocked the Prophet's message about life after death, saying that men of the past had mouldered away, to which Muhammad replied that God is able to restore them to life since he can do anything. At the Judgement every man will have a book handed to him which records his deeds on earth; the good man receives it in his right hand and the bad man in his left and behind his back. False gods will be invoked in vain by unbelievers, and a light or heavy balance of good or evil deeds will decide the future lot (101:5–6).

The result of the Judgement is Paradise or Hell, there is no intermediate state, and each is everlasting. The abode of the blessed is called the Garden (*Jannat*) or Paradise (*Firdaus*). It is the Garden of Eden, or of delight, through which rivers flow. There the blessed enjoy rich clothing, food and celestial wine served by ever-youthful boys. Companions of the blessed are

7

the *houris*, wide-eyed damsels, perhaps like angels. But men, women and children may enter Paradise, and the 'purified spouses', like their husbands, seek the vision of God. The inmates of Paradise are those who have been prayerful and charitable, or have died for the faith, and they praise God constantly.

Those who are condemned at the Judgement go to Gehenna (*Jahannam*), also called the Fire and the Pit. It is vividly described in contrast to the joys of Paradise, and there are distinctively Arabian features, such as the inmates being given hot water to drink and bitter fruit from a tree, while other descriptions resemble those of Zoroastrian, Jewish and Christian mythology. Hell has seven gates, guarded by nineteen angels, and spiritual beings are sent to administer punishment. The inhabitants of the Fire call to those in the Garden for water, but God forbids it to unbelievers. Hell is full of men and evil spirits (*jinn*), but it has an open mouth to ask if there are any more.

Such pictorial accounts of life after death, as in other religions, served to illustrate sermons and exhortations to the good life by warning of the recompense for sin. Such notions developed over the centuries in popular myths, but it is uncertain how literally they were taken. The great theologian Ghazali in the twelfth century considered some of the descriptions of the future life to have a chiefly moral meaning, and they served to emphasize the importance of the 'straight path' by which God conducts the faithful.

c) Baha'i Faith

The Baha'is, whose teachers lived chiefly in Muslim lands, had both similar and distinctive ideas of death. Death is fixed by God, and for the righteous it is a return to the heavenly home and reunion with God. The stages that mark the wayfarer's journey from this abode of dust to the heavenly homeland are said to be Seven Valleys or Seven Cities, and passing through these the traveller gains the ocean of nearness and union and drinks of the peerless wine. All men, after their physical death, shall estimate the worth of their deeds, and realize all that their hands have wrought. Those that are the followers of the one true God shall experience indescribable joy and gladness, but

8

those who live in error shall be seized with fear and trembling and filled with a consternation that nothing can exceed.

d) Christianity

Christian teaching from the beginning was distinctive in its faith in the resurrection of Jesus Christ, and the early Christians are said to have preached both 'Christ and him crucified' and 'Jesus and the resurrection'. The problems which had troubled thinking men in the Old Testament as to why the righteous suffered became even more acute at the crucifixion of Jesus, but they were suddenly transformed by faith in his resurrection and they were problems no more. Early Christians suffered and were persecuted, but they always had before them the example of the saints of the past, as described in Hebrews 11, and they toiled on especially 'looking unto Jesus'.

That Jesus really died is affirmed by all four evangelists and throughout the New Testament and Christian history. Stories of his death on the cross include his giving up his spirit and the piercing of his side with a spear so that blood and water came out. The Apostles' Creed continues this affirmation in sharp successive words, 'crucified, dead, buried, descended into Hades'. The resurrection is equally affirmed, not only in the gospels, but also in the account given by Paul in 1 Corinthians 15, with lists of those who were witnesses of the appearances, and affirmation that 'if the dead are not raised, neither has Christ been raised; and if Christ has not been raised, your faith is vain, you are still in your sins.'

For ordinary people death was also a fact, as Hebrews said again (9:27), 'it is appointed unto men once to die, and after that the judgement.' But early Christians spoke of death as sleep. When Stephen had been stoned, he prayed to the Lord to receive his spirit and not blame his persecutors, 'and when he had said this, he fell asleep.' Similar confidence in continuing life is found at many periods of church history, as in the eighteenth century hymn which said, 'Rejoice for a brother deceased, our loss is his infinite gain.'

A theology of death was worked out by Paul (1 Cor. 15), parts of which have remained in use in funeral services ever since. Death is connected with our first parents, 'as in Adam all die ' for the first man was earthy and we bear his image. But

9

eternal life comes through Christ, since 'the second man is the Lord from heaven,' and 'in Christ all shall be made alive.' Paul's teaching on the 'spiritual body' would have saved the church a lot of trouble if it had been developed. He made a comparison with a seed of corn which grows up as a blade of wheat, and similarly what dies is a natural body and what is raised is a spiritual body. 'Flesh and blood cannot inherit the kingdom of God, neither does corruption inherit incorruption,' but 'this mortal must put on immortality.'

Unfortunately the Apostles' Creed later declared a belief in 'the resurrection of the flesh' (*sarx*, conveniently mistranslated in the English Prayer Book as 'body'). The Thirty-nine Articles of the Church of England affirmed this notion of Christ also, who was said to have taken again 'his body, flesh, bones . . . wherewith he ascended into heaven.'

Pictures of heaven and hell in Christian mythology were partly influenced by Zoroastrian and Jewish ideas, and Revelation was particularly instrumental in propagating descriptions of the throne of God in heaven, a sea of glass in front of it, and round it four creatures full of eyes and wings, like the cherubim described in Ezekiel 1. The New Jerusalem was to be cubic, with equal walls and gates, many jewels, and trees and waters of life. Similarly hell was a bottomless pit, where Satan was bound with his angels. Once again such imagery was not all taken literally. It is not just a modern discovery that God is not 'up there' on a cloud surrounded by saints playing harps. As early as the third century the great Alexandrian theologian, Origen, said that such imagery was like a child's picture book, and the same was repeated later by Luther.

The stark contrast between heaven and hell was modified from early centuries by prayers for the dead, common to both eastern Orthodox and western Catholic, and by the doctrine of Purgatory which was developed most systematically in the west. Dante's famous poem *The Divine Comedy*, in the early fourteenth century, conducts the pilgrim through Hell, Purgatory and Paradise. It culminates with the vision of God, the Beatific Vision of the 'love that moves the sun and the other stars.' But mechanical explanations of Purgatory, and the sale of indulgences to remit some future sufferings, led to the rejection of the doctrine by most Protestants. Prayers for the dead have been practised by some, but not at all by many others. Many modern Protestants have believed in 'conditional immortality', which seems to imply some progress in the life after death, or in 'universal restoration'.

2. Wisdom Religions

a) Hinduism

It is sometimes said that the prophetic or Semitic religions teach a linear conception of human progress, in a line rising from low beginnings through one life on earth to perfection in the kingdom of God or heaven. By contrast Indian and far-eastern religions are said to have a cyclic notion, teaching that all things move round in cycles of birth, death and rebirth going on endlessly. This applies to human life and to the whole universe. But the details should not be pushed too far, and it is believed in India that liberation or salvation can be obtained from this cycle or chain or rebirth, into the bliss of an abstract Nirvana.

Indian and similar religions are also said to be world denying as against the world affirming Semitic religions. But Christianity has often taught world denial, and Indian and Chinese religions have inspired great civilizations in this world.

Belief in rebirth (reincarnation or transmigration) is characteristic of Indian and related religions, and while such a belief was held by some of the Greek philosophers it has not generally been accepted in the Semitic and western worlds. It seems likely that rebirth was an ancient Indian belief, for it first appears in the philosophical Upanishads (about 800 BC) as something which had been previously unknown to the Brahmin priests but which was held by the rulers of the land. The texts say that a young Brahmin was asked by a ruler where the dead go, why heaven is not full up, and how they come back into the world. He confessed his ignorance, and so did his father, whereupon they were instructed in the traditional belief that when the dead are cremated some pass into the flame of the fire, rise up to heavenly worlds, and never return. Others pass into the smoke and rise up to the sky but eventually they return in the rain, passing into the earth and into plants, becoming food and being born again to women.

A moral influence in reincarnation appears in the doctrine of *Karma*, deeds and the result of deeds. Those who have done good deeds in this life but are born again will come into a pleasant family of a priest, a warrior or a merchant. But those whose conduct has been evil will be born again as a dog, a pig or an outcaste.

The doctrine of rebirth, and of all survival of death, is based upon the conviction that the soul or self (*atman*) of man is immortal and indestructible. This is taught in the Upanishads, and repeated verbally in two central verses of the Bhagavad Gita. When the warrior Arjuna hesitates on the field of battle because of many people who will be killed and the just order of society overthrown, the god Krishna encourages him with these words, 'The soul never dies and is never born, it did not come into being and will not cease to exist; it is primeval, unborn, eternal, everlasting, and it is not killed when the body is killed.' (2:20)

This idealistic philosophy considers that the soul or spirit is the only reality, it is both pre-existent and post-existent, because it is eternal, uncreated and never destroyed. The soul cannot die even when the body dies, and though it may be associated with many bodies in different rebirths during its journeyings, its true destiny is to get beyond this world into eternity.

Critics of the doctrine of rebirth often say that we have no memory of previous lives, and therefore we cannot profit from them, so that there is neither proof nor advantage. But many stories are told, from India to Japan, of people meeting in the next life who were closely associated in this life, and the Buddha himself at his enlightenment is said to have looked back on all his previous lives. However, in the philosophy of Hinduism the belief in rebirth does not depend on memory, and stories of past lives are never given in evidence there. The foundation for belief in the survival of death and rebirth is the conviction of the eternal soul, which was never born and can never be destroyed.

The great Upanishadic philosopher Yajna-valkya spoke about death in similes. As a heavily loaded cart starts creaking, so the body starts to groan when it is breathing its last, under the weight of its intelligent soul. As a berry, a fig or a mango fruit falls off a tree when it is ripe, so the spirit frees itself from its limbs when it is weakened by old age and it hastens back to the origin of life. As noblemen, policemen, chariot-drivers and village heads gather round a king when he is leaving them, so all the breaths gather round the soul when one is breathing one's last. When a man is dying he does not see, smell, taste, speak, hear, think, touch or know, but by the light of the heart the soul leaves the body and its life goes out. As a caterpillar comes to the end of a blade of grass and draws itself up to take the next step, so the soul leaves the body and draws itself together for the next life.

There are many popular tales in Hinduism about heavens and hells, which may be considered as intermediary places of reward and punishment before the next rebirth. Different gods had their own heavens, for example on the great mythical mountain Meru in the centre of the earth, or in the northern ocean where Vishnu rested on a coiled snake with a thousand heads, or in the solar heaven where Indra ruled over a splendid abode of gods and spirits. Hell was a place of torment, called Naraka, divided into seven or twenty-one levels, and some-times there were said to be eighty-six lower pits full of fire and torture. These places have been popularly believed in by many Hindus, though the wise think of them as pictures to help or warn ordinary people.

b) Sikhism

The Sikhs, who taught the unity of God in contrast to some pantheistic or polytheistic Hindu beliefs, nevertheless retained belief in the deep-rooted Indian notion of rebirth. Guru Nanak spoke of man being born and dying, coming and going in the round of transmigration, and of the release that came by union with the eternal Lord. Man arrives and departs in this life according to the natural way of *Karma*, but those who are devoted to God are emancipated and not bound again. Guru Arjan spoke of becoming insect or animal in different births, and eventually in human form meeting the Lord of the uni-verse. By overcoming ignorance and worldly attachment (*maya*) and obeying the will of God, liberation will come.

c) Buddhism

Buddhism also held and transmitted to other races the belief in rebirth, for Buddhism was the great Indian missionary religion. In the *Questions of King Milinda* the 'round of existence' is described as 'to be born here and to die here, to die here and to be born elsewhere.' But Buddhist belief appears to be more difficult than Hindu because of its negative teaching about the soul and the indefinable state of Nirvana. Gautama the Buddha, about the fifth century BC, taught in his second sermon the 'Marks of No-self' or 'Non-soul'. He said that 'the body is not-soul, for if it were the soul it would not be subject to sickness.' Similarly, feeling, perception, bodily elements and consciousness are not the soul. The Buddha, however, never said that there was no soul, as the doctrine of 'non-self' (*an-atta*) has sometimes been explained today. He said that the soul could not be grasped or apprehended.

As in Hinduism, the condition of rebirth was thought by Buddhists to be determined by *Karma*, and one was linked again with a new body according to the deeds of the past life. The question was then asked whether the one who is reborn is the same as the one who had just died. And the answer was that he is neither the same nor different. It is like a baby, who is not the same as the grown man later, but who develops into him. And it is like the flame of a candle, which is not the same in the last watch of the night as the flame in the first watch, and yet the flames are not separate.

The idea of Nirvana seems to have begun with the Buddhists and the Jains, a smaller contemporary religious and ascetic movement in India. Nirvana is not mentioned in the Hindu philosophical Upanishads, which were composed shortly before and perhaps during early Buddhism, but Hindus soon adopted the word and it appears in the Bhagavad Gita. Before that time, Buddhists and Jains had spoken about Nirvana, deriving the word from the extinction of a flame. Nir-vana means literally out-blown, extinguished, calmed. It is used of a lamp or a fire being blown out, and then of the flame of life and the fires of passion. Sometimes today Nirvana is explained as extinction of the soul, but this notion was never held by the Jains or early Buddhists, for they sought the extinction of all desires in the perfect calm of final bliss.

King Milinda asked the monk who instructed him whether the Buddha still existed, and he was given the categorical answer, 'Yes.' But it was then stated that the Buddha cannot now be located or pointed out, for since he has attained final Nirvana 'it is not possible to point at the Lord and say that he is either here or there.'

The nature of Nirvana was also discussed, saying that it is absolute ease and one cannot point out its form or shape, its duration or size. Comparisons may be made, however, for as a medicine brings an end to sickness, so Nirvana ends suffering and gives security. Like a wishing-jewel, Nirvana grants all that one can desire and it gives joy and light. As a mountain peak is inaccessible, so Nirvana is beyond all passions, for seeds cannot grow there as they cannot grow on the top of a mountain. Nirvana is unspoiled, like a lotus flower untouched by the mud in which it grows, and as cool water allays fever and quenches thirst, so does Nirvana.

This is advanced spiritual teaching, but for ordinary people there were descriptions of heavens and hells in popular literature. Although early Buddhism did not teach belief in a supreme God, there were plenty of other gods in the stories and they appear as messengers or subordinates to the Buddha. These were Hindu gods such as Vishnu, Indra and Brahma, whose images are still found in many Buddhist temples. The Buddha himself was called 'teacher of gods and men', and the 'god above the gods', so that he was functionally the Supreme Being. He came down from the Tushita heaven, say the scriptures, for his last appearance on earth, having passed through some five hundred and fifty births before his final Nirvana.

The heavens were described as full of beautiful beings, with fragrant robes and garlands, trees covered with fruits and flowers, pools with golden lilies, musical instruments of many kinds, birds with brilliant plumage, and nymphs in the prime of youth. In contrast the hells are ruled by demons who tie up the damned with ropes, drive hot stakes through them, trim them with hatchets, drag them across blazing fires, and so on ever more dreadfully. However the pains of hell are not ever-lasting, and when evil deeds are purged the souls may rise again to other chances on earth. Similarly the heavens are not eternal, but when merit is exhausted the gods and other beings have more lives to pass through till they finally attain to the liberation of Nirvana.

d) China and Japan

Taoism and Confucianism were the two most important native teachings of ancient China, with Buddhism coming from India to make a powerful third doctrine. Taoist philosophy was mystical and poetical and the *Tao Te Ching*, 'the classic of the Way and its Power', teaches the great principle of the indefinable Way which underlies all life, human and other. 'To be one with the Way is to endure for ever, and such a one, though his body perish, is never exposed to danger.' The second great writing of the Taoist school, the *Chuang Tzu*, about the third century BC taught a happiness which is beyond life and death. Indeed it almost glorifies death in a morbid fashion, as rest after labour and the cure of the sickness of life.

Later religious Taoism developed occult movements which sought for immortality through divination and magic. There was a great deal of mythology and alchemy, superstitions and secret societies. Today much of popular Taoism is almost defunct, at least in mainland China, but Taoism greatly influenced Chinese thought with its teaching of a good life on earth, harmony with nature, bodily and spiritual health, simplicity and peace of mind.

From early times the Chinese believed in the existence of nature spirits and spirits of ancestors who needed to receive sacrifice. The ancestors were thought to continue some kind of collective existence in heaven, and sacrifies to them were essential for the welfare of the family and clan. Confucius, in the sixth century BC, is said to have revived or purified the ritual for the dead, and to have told children to mourn three years for their deceased parents. Confucius himself came to be venerated as the 'Primal Sage' and the 'Teacher of Ten Thousand Generations', and for three centuries after his death emperors went to bow at his grave. In modern times, under communist government, his teachings have been criticized, but also at times his grave has been repaired.

The dead were commemorated in China by setting up tablets bearing their names in special rooms, and as the tablets of new members arrived the older ones were put in collective ancestral halls. In both cases the tablets were tended by elderly or poor people, and had candles and incense sticks burning before them. These halls were not temples, though sometimes they included images, and Buddhist and Taoist temples were separate buildings. Confucius and his disciples were worshipped at times, but reformers removed the images and replaced them by carved and gilded tablets like those of other ancestors.

Buddhism appeared in China about the first century AD, and while many people liked it, others criticized it for several reasons. The Buddhist practice of taking young men as monks was disliked by many Chinese because it weakened the family and prevented the offering of sacrifices by sons to their dead fathers. Buddhism introduced the idea of reincarnation, which seemed to deny the existence of the ancestors who must have been born again on earth. A Chinese writer, Wang Ch'ung, at this time attacked the belief in a conscious life after death. He did not deny the existence of ghosts but said that 'man lives because of his vital force and when he dies this force is extinguished.' The ancestors were revered in communal family rites but not as individual souls. Death was a natural and welcome release from life and there was no question of a continued rebirth. Chinese Buddhists, like Mou Tzu, replied that 'only the body decays. The spirit never perishes.' He said that the body is like the roots and leaves of grains which die, but the seeds and kernels remain to bring forth new life.

One of the most popular forms of Buddhism in China and Japan was the Pure Land, which taught faith in Amitabha or Amida Buddha who dwelt in the Pure Land or Western Paradise, the Buddha-fields of the western mountains, like the Shangri-la of James Hilton's *Lost Horizon*. All those who had faith in Amida would be born again into his Pure Land, which was described in glowing terms as having terraces, palm trees, bells, jewels, lakes, lotus-flowers, swans, peacocks, and heavenly instruments praising Buddhist doctrine. Blessed Buddhas were there who spoke the languages of the Buddhist countries and they called all beings to them in the bliss beyond the troubles of earthly life. In contrast there would be hells with fires and molten rocks, and beings who would suffer for thousands of years until their evil *Karma* was worked out.

In Tibet a monk would read from the *Book of the Dead* giving instructions to a dying person as to what would come to him on his journey. At the moment of death there would appear brilliant light from which the person would want to flee, but he should submerge himself into it. A few days after death an illusory dream-body would appear, as the result of past bodily energies. Then shining Buddhas would appear and one should dwell in their realms, otherwise angry deities would bring fear and trouble. Faith in the Buddhas would bring salvation, merging 'into the heart of the divine Father-Mother.' But if one fails to grasp the meaning of this, then one is doomed to rebirth and judgement by the King of the Dead according to past deeds. However 'it is you yourself who pronounce your own judgement, which in its turn determines your next rebirth.'

In Japan there was a similar distinction and mingling of the ancient religion with Buddhism, as in China, Shinto, the 'way of the gods', taught that there was a land of death under the earth, and in myths some of the gods were said to have gone there. But modern Shinto teachers, like Hirata, have declared that while the body goes to the land of death the spirit goes to heaven. 'After a man's death the water and earth in him become his corpse, which is left behind, but the soul flies off with the air and fire. This is because fire and air belong to the sky, just as surely as earth and water belong to the ground'.

In Japanese Bushido, 'the way of the warrior', a stern discipline and fearless regard for death was inculcated. In the nineteenth century Shoin was executed for demanding reform and return to traditional Shinto ideals. He said that 'the warrior must keep death constantly before him and have ever in mind that the one death which he has to give must not be suffered in vain. . . If the body dies it does no harm to the mind, but if the mind dies one can no longer act as a man.' Such stoicism allowed the practice of ritual suicide (*seppuka*, or *hara-kiri*), which was adopted by the warriors when they had no alternative but to die.

Buddhism arrived in Japan about the sixth century AD and after initial struggles it made rapid progress. It has become entwined with Japanese life and culture, so that many people go to both Shinto and Buddhist shrines. A shrine like the Yasukuni in Tokyo, which commemorates all the dead, includes Shinto and Buddhist styles in its architecture. Even those who commit ritual suicide under the principles of Shinto or Confucianism, are strengthened by Buddhist beliefs in a better future life when, for example, husband and wife or separated lovers may meet again. Shinto performs life-giving ceremonies for children and wedding couples, while Buddhism takes care of nearly all the funerals, with cremations and family memorials performed with recitations of Buddhist texts.

3. Conclusion

Not only is belief in the survival of death very ancient, it is also widespread and enduring. We have seen that this belief appears in many forms and it is shaped by the prevalent doctrines of the religion in question. It has many varieties and myths, but there is no doubt that the funeral ceremonies of all peoples have contained statements which imply an existence beyond the grave.

In modern times some of these past beliefs may appear to be difficult, if not incredible, and with a decline of religious practice in some countries acute problems arise. Do those who attend funeral services accept all the doctrines of the ritual which is performed? Yet they almost invariably wish for a religious service, and they would find it hard to suggest alternatives. Religious statements are pictorial, suggesting beliefs by imagery rather than defining them logically, and their very antiquity may be an advantage when dealing with subjects that are beyond daily experience.

One of the great changes over the past few centuries has been rapidly increasing urbanisation. In cities men and women are largely out of touch with nature, though the craze for gardening shows that they need it. Further we are shielded from some of the harsher facts of life. Babies are born in hospital, the sick are sent there, and the insane are put into asylums. Death often takes place in hospital and the relatives may not see the corpse, and even at home the undertaker comes quickly and takes it away. In the past, and in country places today, men and women have been closer to the natural events of life and death, and to see the sick and dying was commonplace. Wars, invasions and slavery brought countless people to see corpses such as only appear on our television screens. In the light of such facts, religious beliefs developed since remotest antiquity, and they are still deeply held by those who live the most natural life.

Yet we are all aware that life is something more than suburban commuting. 'Reality,' wrote a scientist, 'is not only more fantastic than we think, but also much more fantastic than anything we can imagine.' A great new fact of modern times is the knowledge we have of the beliefs of other religions than our own, which was not available to our forefathers. These religions reveal the agelong concern of mankind with life and death and life beyond death. They may help to bring, as Wordsworth put it.

Faith in life endless, the sustaining thought
Of human being, Eternity, and God.

Children Understanding Death
by Brian Gates

It is difficult enough to speak of an adult's understanding of death and what may lie beyond, but it is even more difficult to speak of a child's understanding. For both, many different levels are involved.

As adults we are conscious that people die and that one day this must happen to us. For much of the time, we probably live in expectation of at least the biblical 'three score years and ten', but at the same time we know there are threats to this which prompt the purchase of life insurance policies. In some respects these threats are so certain that they can even be mapped in an atlas of mortality.

In addition to any consciousness of biological and social facts about death, there is also a less conscious awareness of what is happening. Deep down we know we are dying – eventually. This fact flickers in and out of our consciousness, brought to light perhaps by the death of a close friend, a motorway pile-up, or some incident in a television play. Psychologists make much of the presence of death in our unconscious lives and of its effect on our behaviour. It may well explain why we find 'sick' jokes funny, and perhaps why doctors reputedly have the bawdiest sense of humour.

As adults also we know very well that people hold different views about death and the prospect of some beyond to it. It is less than a century since cremation was made lawful in England. Few of the then strident Christian theological objections to it are still heard, but there is no doubt that many remain suspicious of it, not least among Catholics and Muslims. We are aware of these beliefs, as of the elaborate funerary routines reported from America, or the occasional oddity of a casket being buried under the goal mouth at the home team's football ground. Equally, we know that some believe that rotting is the end of life, or that there is new life in heaven, hell, or as a result of being born again into this or another world. We also know what our own personal beliefs are in this regard; maybe clear, maybe muddled, but certainly our own personal equation.

Children's understandings are no less complex. They too are aware of the fact of death, more often than not from before going to school. It is very difficult for them not to have met the death of a grandparent, neighbour, television acquaintance or pet animal. Younger children may even show great interest in the mechanics of dying – staggering to a collapse, eyes popping and so on. Yet even without direct contact with funerals or cemeteries there may be with them too an unconscious sense of dying, or at least potential loss of being.

This is the thrust of an experience described by James Britton:

Alison, at the age of six and a half, took to watching her father go down the road in the mornings until he was right out of sight. One morning, after doing this faithfully for a couple of weeks, she left the window and went into the kitchen and explained to her mother, 'You see, I hate seeing things going away – even the bath-water.' Well, certainly the bath-water does go away, and some infants sometimes are distressed that it does. But Alison at six was dredging a long way back in her experience to bring this to light. Perhaps from infancy it had stood for 'things that go away and don't come back.' Like most young children she had not been easily comforted when lost or broken things were replaced by others even when they were so like the originals that she could not have told the difference. No doubt children have to learn from experience what are the possibilities, the limits of experience (and even, in due course, the probabilities, the odds for and against); they have to learn from experience what things go away and come back and what things go away and don't come back. There is no doubt that at the level of conscious expectations Alison knew her father would come back. But the uncertainty of her infancy, still alive, must have found expression in this situation – hence the need for a long, last look every morning. What her comment that morning attempted, then, may have been a deep-seated adjustment, the laying of a doubt about the world, rather than the interpretation of a daily occurrence. At all events, the morning ritual was no longer necessary and was soon given up and forgotten. (*Language and Learning*, pp. 73–4)

Adah Maurer makes similar claims for the significance of young children's play where they deliberately delight in throwing toys down, or hiding themselves away, provided all can very soon be made to re-appear. From our observations of children's play and singing rhymes we may well recognise some apprehension of the precariousness of life coming through. A developing consciousness of death is therefore likely to be part of the experience a child brings to school. This is illustrated by the following extract from a conversation with six year old Cheryl:

Girls are not allowed to go to funerals, they are really not allowed, because otherwise they could cry and they could think how sad it is and they can spoil themselves and it is too dangerous.
Why is it too dangerous?
Well, just in case you think of it and you think it is really you are dead, yourself.
Does everybody die?
No, not everybody, only if you don't eat, if you don't feel well or if your heart stops beating for a few minutes, you die.
When do people die?
When they don't eat anything for a few days, say 50 days.
Just old people?
Well, if you have something to eat everyday, say breakfast, say 3 times a day you won't die.
Ever?
Well, if you never have one; you don't die for one day without food.
You will never die?
No, until you stop for a few days.
Do children ever die?
Well, no, no because their mothers always give them something to eat.
Do they ever get knocked down by a car?
Ah, now, if they don't look for their safety, they don't look right and left and listen, they can go by with a car coming. They can die, really, because a wheel can go over them and they just fall.
And what happens then?
Well, an ambulance comes, that is the time for an ambulance comes, do do, do, do, to bib everything out of the way.

And what happens when you die?
Well you have to get buried, because when you put your head under the blankets you suffocate and you stop breathing, so they put you in a suffocating thing so they know you are dead now, they put them suffocating.
Does everybody suffocate and die?
Well, only if they think they are allowed to go under the blankets, right under and stay under over night then they can suffocate.
Do all old people die?
Well not in fact all of them, if they still have something to eat.
Then they are all right?
Yes.
So, how old can you be?
Well, you can go up to, well, 30 or 40 or 50 but not up to 100, that's now allowed, no-one can go up to 100.
Can they not? So they have to die before they are 100?
Yes, or 99. Nothing after that.
But does everybody have to die?
Well, when they get old nearly to a 100 they have to die.
Do they?
Yes, because they get old and soggy and all horrible and they get throats and heart attacks and they die, but sometimes when you have operations you die, because it can be that your heart has no beat in it.
Is that the end of them?
Yes, they are finished then.
And they don't come back to life again?
No, they never, or it is never true that they can come back to life when they are really dead, it is never true. They just can't stop their heart, their heart is just as still as nothing.

In places it is almost as though she can be seen working her way through to and perhaps articulating for the first time, the full facts of death.

Children of this age are not only factually aware, they are forging their beliefs on the question of any beyond to death. Cheryl, for whatever reasons, expressly rejects this prospect. Anne, another 6 year old in the same class affirms without hesitation that:

When you are buried, the air in you comes out and it goes up to heaven . . . you go up by steps.

She knows this because her dad has told her, but apparently neither of them is sure why there are steps. If statements of belief are available for younger children, then so too are they for their older brothers and sisters, as we shall see.

Differences of belief abound, even between children from similar religious backgrounds. In quoting other individual conversations there is therefore no intent to suggest that any of them is totally typical or representative of the tradition from which they come, though some hallmarks of the parent faith are usually there. As well as diversity in expressions of the content of belief, there are wide variations in the strength of belief, almost irrespective of their formal religious label.

Variations in strength of belief in a beyond to death among a sample of children (aged 6–15 yrs.) from different religious background in English schools

	Strong	Reservations (pro)	Reservations (con)	Rejecting
Anglican	68.5	12	13.5	6
Unattached	48.5	15.5	11.5	24.5
Non-Conformist	76.5	13	8	2.5
Roman Catholic	85	15	–	–
Jewish	56	22	12	10
Sikh	61.5	10.5	7.5	20.5
Muslim	78.5	–	14.5	7

The parent religious community has its orthodox teachings and highly sophisticated interpretations, but children, like adults, may express their own beliefs in a slightly different way from what might be expected given their backgrounds. Children from Christian backgrounds, Protestant, Catholic, and disaffected generally think of a beyond to death in the forms of heaven and hell, but with wide variations in how they are conceptualised and with no shortage of additional or alternative references to spirits, ghosts, and reincarnation. The following extract from nine year old Alan is especially vivid:

Heaven is just happiness, having to know that you haven't got anything dragging around you. There's nothing to stop you from doing anything, you haven't got any laws . . . I think it's a normal family,

25

but we have a ruler; he just doesn't stop you from doing anything. He's called Jesus; he's very just. You die, and it's like being put in prison for a while, while people are judging what you've done, to see what charges they can give you . . . (Jesus) looks back. You might say his memory is like a drawer of files. You might say he looks at what you've done . . . and whether you're going this road, that road, and whether you're going to stay here longer and whether you are going to go up the good road. . . . The idea of going to heaven is that you can see everyone, and you can talk with them, and you can talk as long as you like and there's no need to bother about telephone bills, because it's just natural. No one is working up there; it's just working by nothing. If you turn on the television, you don't have to say the fuse is gone, because the fuse will always be there.

Jewish boys and girls frequently refer to heaven and the soul, but more exceptionally also to mediums and reincarnation. Twelve year old Susanah speaks of the Messianic Israel:

All the Jewish people will go to Israel and the people who are dead will come alive. We don't know if they'll come in their actual bodies or just their souls . . . The world after we die is like a paradise, a Garden of Eden really. When the Messiah comes there won't be any more dying. They will all go to Israel, all the Jewish people, and the Christians and all the Roman Catholics will all go mainly to Jerusalem. And there is a legend that says that Israel will hold everyone that comes there.

Fourteen year old Jacob translates this as leisure:

When you look at dying I consider it is the best thing that could happen to a man, because when you look at life, a person is born, he goes through his life with all the pressures of his life and then he comes to the end of his life as a man and I tend to associate this with relaxation, eternal relaxation. I believe the spirit goes and is in heaven and is in paradise. Sometimes I associate heaven with being in the upmost limits of space. Sometimes I associate it with being in the mind. Sometimes to me it is memory of dead people, people that I can remember, not the fact that they lived but the fact that their memory lives, but I am not sure at all. I have been trying to find out myself.

Muslim boys and girls readily seem to stress the coming Day of Judgement as in the following extract from eleven year old Belgin:

*On the Resurrection Day God calls all the people together and he
tells you, or rather asks you how much wrong and how much right
you have done, have you done more right than wrong. You have
to answer and if you have done more bad than right then you go to
hell and if you have done more right than bad you go to heaven,
you stay in heaven.*
So everybody goes to heaven first?
*No, they go on to a very big kind of field, which is up there and on
the Day of Resurrection he calls you. God gathers you over there
and he tells you because, you see, you have got two angels on your
shoulders and on the left is the one who writes the bad things you
have done and on the right he writes the good things you have
done. You can't see them you can't feel them because they are invisible but they write all the good and bad and then on the Day of
Resurrection they take, they go up there and they show God and
God sees it.*

According to a Muslim boy, slightly older, the difficulty of
passing judgement is made easier by the aid of a video-recorder
with play-back facilities. Some fear for the fate of non-Muslims
or stress the end of inequality in God's new day; even physical
beauty or ugliness will cease to matter.

Children from Sikh families also speak of heaven and hell. but
more substantially, like Hindu children, of reincarnation:

*In the Punjab, some scatter their ashes. I don't know why they
light the body of people but they light it and throw the ashes all
over, over river, you know.*
Why do they throw the ashes over the river?
*It might be he will be born again to somebody and they might rec-
ognise him.*
Might be born again to somebody?
Yes.
What do you mean?
He might have another life, as somebody else.
Do you think that does happen to people that they are born
again?
*Yes, I have heard from my grandmother in India, once they had
scattered the ashes and they had seen the same girl, she was going*

27

to be my aunt, you see, the same girl was seen by my grandmother in the temple, she was just going to say and she fell into tears, at seeing her.

So what happens when they die? Is that the end of them or not?

To some it is the end, to some it is not.

Why to some the end and not others?

Some don't do anything before they die, and some do, like me. You see, I have killed many things, and I have sworn on somebody, things like that. When I die, from what I have heard from my grandmother, when we die we go to heaven.

God, if you have done anything, he pokes some metal things in your eyes, you see. Yes, if you drop salt on the ground, you see, and you don't pick it up when you die. You go to pick it with your eyes, I have heard that from my grandmother.

She told me that he picks out your eyes and, you know, like eyes coming out and still with your face, you see, and the eyes picking up the salt. . . . Instead of poking the metal thing in your eyes. You pick, you hurt yourself for what you have done.

What is this about not all people being born again?

Oh, yes, some do sins you see. Then he doesn't get born again. He is just left, and I don't know actually but, you know, God puts him in another life where there are wild creatures, so that he can be, you know, eaten again. If an animal is killed there, the animal when he dies, he will go up there and if he has done a thing he comes down at the same place and is eaten. If I do a bad thing, if I am born again you see, I will be born into another creature, like an ant, or I have killed many ants, you see, and that ant will kill me, you see, the ant that I have killed, will kill me when I'm an ant. Yes, he will, he will have done the work, he will have taken revenge.

The interspersing with elements of folk belief evident from this fourteen year old Sikh boy are equally forthcoming from every other background. As already hinted such overt references to reincarnation are not confined to children from an Indian religious background. Memories of former lives and sense of *déjà vu* are frequently cited by children of Anglo-Saxon stock, and occasionally belief in reincarnation is the personal credo of a boy or girl who claims to be actively Christian as in the case of this fourteen year old Anglican church-goer:

Soon after you are born again as some other being or animal or anything else – any living thing. You don't 'go' for ever. After all, we are here; we must have come from somewhere else. Why suddenly end a life, and not come again? This seems impossible; when you die, you must be born again. That's what I believe . . . I believe that we were something else before we are now, and I think we continue to be like that for evermore. . . . It could be as differing things, different living things, anything, as a butterfly, you wouldn't know. Like as I continue to be as I am now, the butterfly would continue its life. It wouldn't know anything beforehand or afterhand, like I don't know anything before or after.

Lastly, there are those who reject any possibility of a beyond to death, sometimes in the name of science, which (in spite of science fiction) is claimed to render such belief incredible, or in simple stoic resignation:

We never really discuss death in our family. I've been very ill once or twice, so's my mother, so its something we don't like mentioning, and you daren't mention death near any of my aunts because they've had such a lot of tragic deaths. My great uncle died one Christmas day as he was preparing the Christmas dinner so they don't bother with Christmas dinners any more and my grandmother on my mother's side died after a very long illness when my mother was about 11 years old.
What do you think happens when people die?
I think myself that once you've died you're finished with, people soon forget about you no matter how popular or otherwise you've been during your lifetime. Once you've died you're forgotten very very quickly except if you're the kind of person who likes to remember these things. Some people really enjoy to remember other people's deaths, though I wouldn't, I'd try to forget about a thing like that as soon as it's possible.

From an inquest on such conversations as these, several conclusions emerge. First, as anticipated, the pupils whom we meet in school bear with them conscious and unconscious understandings of death and beyond, and beliefs about dying and living again. These may be limited or highly elaborated, they may be devout or sceptical, but they are certainly real and deserve to be reckoned with.

Secondly, attention to death and what lies beyond is an educational priority area. It is important for boys and girls to have the opportunity to come to understand what beliefs people have in regard to death. They deserve better than the flat-footed or inert treatment given to death in so many projects on Tutankhamen's tomb, which revealed the glitter of gold, but not the fathoming of human life and death that lay behind it. Even the facts of death themselves merit more direct attention in school than they often receive. In their absence, ethical issues regarding, for instance, differential infant mortality rates between countries or facilities for minority burials will scarcely be noticed.

It would be naive to ignore the risks which face the teacher who more deliberately treats the theme of death in school. Precisely because children are aware of the threat of death, and because the concern runs as deep as it does, they can be upset, especially at times of personal loss. Yet to avoid direct references to the subject throughout the compulsory years of schooling would be to opt for an unreal world. In practice many of the references to death that occur may well be incidental, or provoked by some news report from near or far. But there will also be a place for carefully planned project work on death and any future life. In whatever form it is tackled, it will certainly require proper professional sensitivity on the part of the teacher, both to the individual pupils in the class and to the communal realms of conviction and doubt which he will be seeking to share with them.

Teacher and child alike have much to learn from looking at life in the face of death. Perhaps, adapting an old catholic custom, the curriculum should be composed annually with thoughts of mortality! The agenda then in prospect for the schools and families concerned might be full of life.

Bibliography

General background
S. Anthony, *The Discovery of Death in Childhood and After*, Penguin
J. Britton, *Language and Learning*, Penguin

G. Gorer, *Death, Grief and Mourning in Contemporary Britain*, Cresset
E. A. Grollman, *Explaining Death to Children*, Beacon Press
G. M. Howe *et al.*, *National Atlas of Disease and Mortality*, Nelson
A. Maurer, 'Maturation of Concepts of Death' in *British Journal of Medical Psychology* 39:1, 1966
A. Mitchell, *Children's Attitudes towards Death*, Barrie & Rockliff
L. D. Stamp, *Geography of Life and Death*, Fontana

Classroom texts
M. Ball, *Standpoints: Death*, O.U.P.
C. A. Burland, *Myths of Life and Death*, Macmillan
J. Elliott & E. Pain, *Education, Work and Death*, Lutterworth
E. G. Parrinder, *Search for Meaning: Something after Death?* Denholm House

Fiction
J. Coburn, *Anne and the Sand Dobies*, Seabury
Fynn, *Mister God, This is Anna*, Fontana
P. Pearce, *Tom's Midnight Garden*, O.U.P.

The extracts from conversations with children are taken from interviews conducted by the author with boys and girls from different religious backgrounds in English schools. A short account of the research is given in 'Religion in the Child's own Core Curriculum' in *Learning for Living*, Autumn 1977.

PART 2
STATEMENTS
AND EXTRACTS

BAHA'I FAITH

In the sacred scriptures of all religions, two kinds of death are spoken of, physical death and spiritual death. The former is of great importance to all people, yet if the founders of the great religions are to be believed, the latter is of much greater significance.

Before discussing 'death' it must be established what is meant by 'life'. The Baha'i scriptures teach that the human soul comes into existence at the moment of conception, and that man's physical body is never meant to be the end purpose of existence. The Creator has endowed man with latent spiritual powers in addition to his physical faculties. Development of these powers is the purpose of life, for they are the reflections of divine qualities. Baha'u'llah, founder of the Baha'i Faith, explains it as follows:

> From among all created things he hath singled out for his special favour the pure, the gem-like reality of man, and invested it with a unique capacity of knowing him and of reflecting the greatness of his glory. (Gl.p.77)

Man can only develop these powers by following the Teachings of the Prophet of God. Describing the influence of a Prophet, Baha'u'llah says:

> Through the Teachings of this Day Star of Truth every man will advance and develop until he attaineth the station at which he can manifest all the potential forces with which his

33

inmost true self hath been endowed . . . (Gl.p.67)

The awakening of these spiritual powers is referred to as attaining to true life.

Spiritual Life and Death

True life is not the life of the flesh but the life of the spirit. For the life of the flesh is common to both men and animals, but the life of the spirit is possessed only by the pure in heart who have quaffed from the ocean of faith and partaken of the fruit of certitude. (Iq.p.120)

However, man can only develop his latent spiritual powers by wishing to do so.

All that which ye potentially possess, can however be manifested only as a result of your volition. (Gl.p.148)

Spiritual death is the term applied to a person who uses his free will to turn away from spiritual things and busies himself with the things of this world.

Hell and Heaven

Although man may live a long physical life, if he does not attain to 'second' birth here he will arrive in the next life spiritually deprived. This state was referred to symbolically in past religions as hell. Awareness of God comes through recognising his Prophets. This is the awakening of the higher nature in man; it brings true happiness. This state used to be referred to as heaven.

'Heaven and hell are, therefore, not places, but conditions of the soul, and man may experience some of the joys of heaven, which are spiritual joys, or the pains of hell, which consist in being deprived of these joys, even while still in the body; hell being therefore, lack of spiritual development.' (LAD)

The Next Life

Physical death takes place at a time ordained by God. This is a great release, for the physical body is a severe limitation. Baha'u'llah said of the soul:

When it leaveth the body, however, it will evince such ascendancy, and reveal such influence as no force on earth can equal. Every pure, every refined and sanctified soul will be endowed with tremendous power, and shall rejoice with exceeding gladness. (Gl.p.153)

It is not surprising then that Baha'u'llah taught people who have educated their spiritual natures to look forward with great eagerness to the time when they should leave this physical world.

I have made death a messenger of joy unto thee, wherefore doest thou grieve? (HW 32)

Man was never meant to become deeply attached to his body and he can transcend his physical nature even while on earth with the help of the Manifestation of God who educates man's latent spiritual nature.

The Prophets and Messengers of God have been sent down for the sole purpose of guiding mankind to the straight Path of Truth. The purpose underlying their revelation hath been to educate all men, that they may, at the hour of death, ascend, in the utmost purity and sanctity and with absolute detachment, to the throne of the Most High. (Gl.p.156)

Oneness of the Two Worlds

'The world we can see and the invisible worlds are only separated to our human senses. In reality they constitute one universe, the parts of which are interdependent and intimately connected. So all those living on earth, and those who have passed through the change of death, belong to one and the same organism. Separation from those we love is, therefore, a bodily separation only. Between the seen and the unseen there is a constant intercommunication. For those sufficiently sensitised to finer vibrations, this communion may become conscious and definite; while others may remain quite unaware of the vital connection. To the Prophets and many of the saints, intercourse between both worlds is natural and real.' (LAD)

Among spiritual souls there . . . is a communion which is purified from imagination and fancy, an association sanctified from time and place. So it is written in the Gospel that on

35

Mount Tabor, Moses and Elias came to Christ, and it is evident that this was not a material meeting. It was a spiritual condition. Communications such as these are real, and produce wonderful effects in the minds and thoughts of men and cause their hearts to be attracted. (Abdu'l Baha quoted in LAD)

When we are in a receptive condition, or maybe in dreams, when the soul is lightly tethered to the body, messages can reach us from the other world, and are flashed into the waking consciousness.

The Baha'i teachings admit, of course, the reality of certain supernormal psychic faculties, but they offer the warning that intercourse with the departed should not be sought in order to gratify curiosity, or obtain something for ourselves. For Reality is pure spirit, which occupies no space, and assumes no form. The genuine intercourse with the departed, a sure and safe meeting-place, can always be found in a condition of love and prayer – that is, in a spiritual condition. And it is wisest to let latent psychic faculties unfold naturally, as the soul becomes attuned to the higher vibrations of a pure and unselfish life; since the premature development of these powers may interfere with the state of the soul in the ethereal world, where such powers are fully operative.' (LAD)

Recognition of loved ones in the next life is certain, but it will be by their spiritual qualities, not by their physical bodies. Even in physical life we should learn to appreciate people for their spiritual qualities, rather than for their physical attractions and worldly possessions. 'Abdu'l-Baha, son of Baha'u'llah said:

Physical companionship is ephemeral, but heavenly association is eternal. Whenever thou rememberest the eternal and never ending union thou wilt be comforted. (TAB 99)

Prayers for the Departed

Baha'is are enjoined to pray for the so-called dead, and special prayers have been revealed for the purpose; prayers for forgiveness, spiritual enlightenment, happiness and progress. For progress in the next world is still a law of life, and God's mercy is boundless and his ministering angels always near.

> Those who have ascended have different attributes from those who are still on earth, yet there is no real separation. In prayer there is a mingling of station, a mingling of condition. Pray for them, as they pray for you . . . The real and genuine influence is not in this world but in that other. (Abdu'l-Baha quoted in LAD)

So that in either condition prayers ascend to that divine Reality, 'around the sanctuary of whose Prescence circle the souls of all mankind.' (LAD)

Love is the bond which unites all things. It is the universal law governing all worlds, hence we cannot ever be parted from our loved ones and prayer for their progress is a great help for those whose physical bodies are no longer with us. 'Abdu'l-Baha said:

> As we have power to pray for these souls here, so likewise we shall possess the same power in the other world, which is the kingdom of God. Are not all the people in that world the creatures of God? Therefore in that world also they can make progress. (SAQ 269)

Spiritual Evolution

The soul is all pure goodness at the time of conception in the mother's womb, and it is the force which then gives life to the physical body of the child.

> The soul of man is the sun by which his body is illumined and from which it draweth its sustenance and should be so regarded. (Gl.p.154)

The soul being a separate reality from the physical body is not affected by the death of the body, but continues to progress through all the many other worlds of God. It can do this far better when it is freed from the body.

> The soul that hath remained faithful to the Cause of God, and stood unwaveringly firm in his Path shall, after his ascension, be possessed of such power that all the worlds which the Almighty hath created can benefit through him. (Gl.p.160)

'Within the soul and mind of man are involved all those potentialities which will enable him to enjoy eternal life, and the ever progressive unfoldment of his spiritual faculties, as, for instance, within the unpromising little acorn lie enfolded all the potentialities of a mighty oak tree. Motion being an essential law of all existence, in the realm of spirit there can be no static condition, nor is retreat possible; all movement is bound to be, ultimately, towards a state of perfection. The ethereal vehicle or body used by the soul will accord with and be suitable to the sphere of consciousness in which it is functioning.

When the soul attaineth the Presence of God, it will assume the form that best befitteth its immortality, and is worthy of its celestial habitation. (Gl.p.157)

'Such an order could, naturally, not admit of a backward process; as, to make a crude analogy, a butterfly cannot again return to a chrysalis state. But the qualities, certain faculties and memories of the universal or world spirit, are reincorporated, and serve to illumine the minds of freshly created human beings who are born primarily pure. The results of each individual life-experience go to the general enrichment of humanity; while the injustices suffered by so many in this world receive full compensation in the next, in ways beyond our understanding.

'The development of the soul's spiritual faculties being a law of God, it may continue to acquire endless perfections, and for ever evolve through the realms of infinity; yet will such extensions or deepening of consciousness still be made in the state of humanity. It will not attain to that of Deity.

Both before and after putting off this material form, there is progress in perfection, but not in state. There is no other being higher than a perfect man. But man, when he has reached this state can still make progress in perfections but not in state . . . for the human perfections are infinite. For example, the reality of the spirit of Peter, however far it may progress, will not reach to the condition of the reality of Christ; it progresses only in its own environment (or sphere). ('Abdu'l-Baha)

'Human souls, therefore, do not become God. The creatures

38

cannot become their Creator.' (LAD)

Know thou of a truth that the soul, after its separation from
the body, will continue to progress until it attaineth the presence of God, in a state and condition which neither the revol-
ution of ages and centuries, nor the changes and chances of
this world, can alter. It will endure as long as the Kingdom of
God, his sovereignty, his dominion and power will endure. It
will manifest the signs of God and his attributes, and will
reveal his loving kindness and bounty. The movement of my
pen is stilled when it attempteth to befittingly describe the
loftiness and glory of so exalted a station. The honour with
which the Hand of Mercy will invest the soul is such as no
tongue can adequately reveal, nor any other earthly agency
describe. Blessed is the soul which, at the hour of its separation from the body, is sanctified from the vain imaginings of
the peoples of the world. Such a soul liveth and moveth in
accordance with the Will of its Creator, and entereth the all-
highest Paradise . . . If any man be told that which hath
been ordained for such a soul in the worlds of God, the Lord
of the throne on high and of earth below, his whole being will
instantly blaze out in his great longing to attain that most
exalted, that sanctified and resplendent station . . .
(Gl.pp.155–156)

Prayer

O my Lord! I myself and all created things bear witness unto
thy might and I pray thee not to turn away from thyself this
spirit that hath ascended unto thee, unto thy heavenly place,
thine exalted Paradise and thy retreats of nearness.

O thou who art the Lord of all men! Grant then, O my God,
that thy servant may consort with thy chosen ones, thy saints
and thy Messengers in heavenly places that the pen cannot
tell nor the tongue recount.

O my Lord, the poor one hath verily hastened unto the
Kingdom of thy wealth, the stranger unto his home within

thy precincts, he that is sore athirst to the heavenly river of thy bounty. Deprive him not, O Lord, of his share of the banquet of thy grace or of the favour of thy bounty. Thou art in truth the Almighty, the Gracious, the All-Bountiful.

O my God, thy trust hath been returned unto thee. It behoveth thy grace and thy bounty that have compassed thy dominions on earth and in heaven, to vouchsafe unto thy newly welcomed one thy gifts and thy bestowals, and the fruits of the tree of thy grace! Powerful art thou to do as thou willest. There is none other God but thee, the Gracious, the Most Bountiful, the Compassionate, the Bestower, the Pardoner, the Precious, the All-Knowing.

I testify, O my Lord, that thou hast enjoined upon men to honour their guest, and he that hath ascended unto thee, hath verily reached thee and attained thy Presence. Deal with him then according to thy grace and bounty! By thy Glory, I know of a certainty that thou wilt not deny thyself from that which thou hast commanded thy servants, nor wilt thou deprive him that hath clung to the cord of thy bounty and hast ascended to the Day-Spring of thy wealth.

There is none other God but thee, the One, the Single, the Powerful, the Omniscient, the Bountiful.

References

Gl.   *Gleanings from the Writings of Baha'u'llah*
Iq.   *Kitab-i-Iqan*, Baha'u'llah
HW   *Hidden Words*, Baha'u'llah
TAB   *Tablets of Abdu'l-Baha*
LAD   *Life After Death*, Florence E. Pinchon
SAQ   *Some Answered Questions*, Abdu'l-Baha

The prayer is taken from *Baha'i Prayers for Special Occasions*. This and the other works listed are published by the Baha'i Publishing Trust.

BUDDHISM

The Buddha was not a far, remote being, a God or a mystery; religion was for him not an enigmatic abstraction from reality or a philosophy too severe for ordinary men to follow. He was a man who lived among men and women, totally concerned with people, their experiences and their problems. Wherever he went there were always men and women of all kinds crowding to see him. They brought him their questions and problems, their joys and griefs. Some came to test him, some to quarrel, and many came just to sit with him, to absorb his extraordinary calm and loving awareness.

Though he was a man, he knew men with insight like a God. He had himself stepped very close to death – once alone, in a wild and dangerous jungle, deserted by his friends, experiencing utter solitude and starvation. The Buddha knew death and found within himself resources to deal with the accompanying fear, sorrow, pain and mourning and to overcome death itself. Seeing through the change that is death he perceived loving wisdom that is wholly living and wholly peaceful, wholly self-reliant and wholly compassionate.

The man who was born in history to the family Gotama became that loving wisdom. He became Buddha – enlightened. He did not then choose to die – he lived with full devotion to the many needs of men and women until he was old. In the end, his body ceased to move. Who can say what then became of his wisdom? He left his teaching and that remains for every Buddhist to make a sincere effort to carry it out day by day in this very life. When we gain that utterly peaceful, loving and generous understanding, then we also are in the state called Buddha – an enlightened one.

Being a man his body was bound for death. This the Buddha accepted. He knew that everything that is born is undergoing a process of change and must die – father, mother, friends – all must one day die. This is the problem which the man Gotama set out to solve and in doing so attained the state of Buddhahood. He then worked for 45 years to show men and women how to *understand* and *live* even in the presence of death.

As children, and often as adults, we sometimes try to forget death; but at times an inner fear or dread comes like an eclipse, or suddenly we are face to face with death, in a road accident or in the sickness and passing away of a friend or loved one.

The Buddha experienced this too, even before he became enlightened. While out walking for pleasure on a bright and happy day, he turned a corner and came suddenly across a corpse on a stretcher, his own glowing young face confronting that grey still mask. He was deeply shocked. He went home, his whole mind and body protesting the claims of life and health and joy – but there was sickness, there was old age, there was death. And not only death, but the mourners – a wife weeping, a partner not knowing how to carry on with his work alone. A ring lay on one of the dead fingers, the hair was beautifully brushed . . . there was separation and loss.

Gotama, the young man who was to become the Enlightened Teacher, or Buddha, was not afraid. What he felt was a great impulse of compassion. He did not run away, he went forward wanting to teach himself and all of us to understand death and to live in the presence of death in the noblest way.

Everything that comes to be must change, that is certain. He saw that the first step in growing up about death is to understand our feelings about it. Each day dies and night is born. Summer, winter, autumn, spring – there is no plant and no creature, no thing at all in this world which does not change. It is our selfish longing for what we may lose which makes us think of death as a sudden absolute end. But really, death is an essential part of life, and death and birth are around us, are active in us, at every instant.

Look at our own bodies – if the skin and flesh and muscle did not die and fall away, we would be trapped in an infant's form. In the body, a million births and deaths take place at every moment. The body is a miracle of rebirth in which our habits, our likes and dislikes, our hunger, and our states of mind are always driving the body towards change and development. Never for an instant does the body cease to die, cease to be born. We might say that we live through life and death at every moment.

Look at the mind. Is there ever a moment of stillness there? Never without change, the mind is a restless complex stream of experiences. Watch your feelings – see how pleasure and discomfort, joy and discontent come one after the other. Memories come and go, ideas are there and vanish, likes and dislikes, plans, purposes – all like waves rising and falling on a stream. We are not only living but dying now, at this and every moment.

The Buddha taught his followers not to fear death, but to know that death and life are two phases of one process. He taught his followers, therefore, to go forward in their lives with great confidence, energy and calm. As we turn to live each moment, we can become aware of what death is and does. We can even learn to care for those in sorrow, those who feel bewilderment at separation and loss.

In a way this is mere common sense as far as the life of the body is concerned. We know very well that the body changes; that its cells die and grow; that it is a stream of energy. But there is more.

We know that those processes can be understood. We can, by good sense and wisdom, or alternatively by blind greed and foolishness, influence and control the body. The body we now possess is the direct result of the exercise, diet and sleep given to it in the preceeding years, months and days. We can by wisdom and other mental qualities control the nourishment of food, exercise and sleep. We can influence the body very much by mental calm and joyfulness, or by tension and desire.

Therefore, if we wish to influence the body to develop as a healthy, skilful, joyful basis for life, then we must be able to control our minds. The mind also grows by what it feeds on; its inclinations cannot be altered easily or suddenly. We contain deep rooted habits, difficult to work on and control with our mind so erratic and self-willed. And yet through good sense and our understanding, we can give the mind correct nourishment to grow in a positive direction.

The Buddha developed a gradual path of self-training, in which he taught the way to come to terms with the deep rooted tendencies and mental habits with which we have to live at the moment of life and also at the moment of death. The path of training begins by developing the confidence and strong ambition to make our speech and actions and thoughts more loving, more compassionate, more *aware*. It begins by not going to extremes; by not indulging to the point of intoxication or addiction; by not rejecting all the good things which enable us to protect our families and create a good society.

In particular, the Buddha saw that our minds are never empty. If we don't *live* – if we don't put ourselves to work, at each moment exercising some care, living fully and caringly – then greed and hatred and lazy doubt rush in. This is the real death. The old must die if the new is to grow. Death after death is birth after birth. As the body dies, at that moment there is birth.

However, the mind does not change in the same way as does the body. Today someone can remember, can see clearly now in his mind's eye, his own home, dear to him as it was forty years ago. The body that saw that house is utterly perished – the skin flakes off, the cells reconstitute, the food is transformed or ejected and the hair and nails wear away. Another body lives now. But still his mind can visit that memory. Can longing and attachment grow from life to life? The mind is urging us to live, to live on. It is the very source of our bodily life – this mind urges us to eat, to learn, to feel, to touch, to see, to die – and to be born. As long as this deep longing goes on, so long are we definitely bound to life and death again and again.

Now we can see that when a Buddhist hears that someone has died, he sees it as being natural and as something that has happened according to the way things happen. He may be as grieved as anyone else to see that person has gone, but his grief is just a longing for the departed person, really a selfish feeling. It is better, the Buddhist believes, to think of that departed person as a traveller. From the death of one life another rises, and we travel together.

The Buddhist sees a world where everything gives rise to a result. Therefore, Buddhists seek to create always a state of mind which is a little purer, a little wiser, a little more loving. That force of goodness which is the well-developed mind will not die, will live on in new forms, ever developing, like all the forms of life we know.

If a Buddhist wishes to bury the departed with some ceremony, he is free to do that, as an expression, perhaps, of his

44

feeling of love towards the departed. He may invite monks to attend the ceremony and a monk will preach a sermon and recite some of the Buddha's teachings on death. But to the Buddhist, that dead body is an empty thing. The Buddhist turns from the dead matter of the body to attend to life, to develop life to the highest, to strive to assist all other beings, his fellow travellers in the process of death and birth.

The Buddhist, in attending to life, is aspiring to walk the road that leads to complete freedom from the fear of death. When, having attained the state of absolute emancipation in this life, on the occurrence of death no further life arises, then we have made an end with noble peace of mind.

Essentially freedom from the fear of death comes from right understanding and giving, leading us to develop the moral conduct, awareness and wisdom that encourage highest service both to ourselves and to others.

In the end, men can achieve an absolute freedom and joy which can be influenced by neither good nor evil, a loving wisdom which is infinite, unaffected by need or longing and free from both life and death.

If we are to understand the attitude of Buddhists to death, we need to enter, at least for a while, a very different world from that in which we are accustomed to live.

In our western, Christian-based culture, we take it for granted, explicitly or implicitly, that we each have a soul, created at some time between conception and birth, which exists independently of other souls, and which is destined for an eternity of happiness or misery as a result of this brief life on earth. No such idea exists in Buddhism.

Buddhists believe that we consist of five constituents, all of which are in a state of flux, and which continually change as a result of several factors. These constitutents are: (1) body or form, *rupa*; (2) sensation or feeling, *vedana*; (3) perception or personal experience of feelings, *sanjna*; (4) impulses or tendencies developed as a result, *sanskara*; (5) consciousness, *vijnana*.

An examination of these components, known as the *skandhas*, reveals that none of them is permanent or unchanging, hence the Buddhist doctrine of *anatma*, or no permanent 'soul'. This is not, as erroneously put about by some earlier and less well-instructed Buddhists, a suggestion of 'soullessness', but a clear indication that our 'souls' are neither separate from those of all other people, nor permanent possessions of our own. They are, like everything else in the realm of birth and death (*sangsara*), changing and impermanent.

So there is no question of 'saving' our individual soul from a world such as this one and having it booked, so to speak, for a permanent realm of happiness or misery hereafter. We are developing, or perhaps allowing ourselves to become retrograde, all the time.

Connected with this belief is that of a continuation of our life of birth and death (*sangsara*) in accordance with our behaviour, so that we accept the idea of rebirth in this plane. We do this because we also understand that the law of action and reaction (*karma*) operates here, and what a man sows that shall he also reap, now or in a later life. But a finite cause can only have a finite result, and to us it would be monstrously unjust, and not in accordance with the discernable pattern of things, if we were to be precipitated into an eternity of happiness or suffering as a result of one short life on earth, where very unequal opportunities determine the lives of everybody.

We feel that Justice would be outraged if a person born here in miserable circumstances, and with limited or indeed damaged faculties, were to be judged solely on one unfortunate lifetime, just as it would be monstrously unjust that any being should be thrown into a short life of suffering at the arbitrary whim of a god. What sort of a supernatural being would deliberately inflict a life of pain and suffering on anyone without any previous cause? In other words how could a person be born deformed, with a damaged brain or body, condemned to a life of pain or deprived of opportunity to lead a full life for any reason, just at the pleasure of a god, and without any previous life which could explain or cause such a happening?

To Buddhists, therefore, we live many lives, and the causes built up in one carry over to the next, which explains the very evident inequalities of physical body and talents which obtain all over this world. We do not suppose these are handed out by a god, since such a being would be more deserving of censure than worship, but are the result of *karma*.

So we have to accept the position as it is now, and build a better future. We try to work with the eternal laws which we observe are in operation, and to improve life for ourselves and all others at the same time. We aim to overcome the limitations of *sangsara* and attain the realm of *Nirvana*, or freedom from the limitations which restrict us now. These two worlds, that of *sangsara* and that of *Nirvana* are not, in the last analysis, separate and unrelated ones, but they interpenetrate. It is our own lack of vision which confines us in the one and prevents us from realising the other.

It will be seen from the above that death is not the end of life, but rather a part of the life-and-death state (*sangsara*) which persists so long as we fail to achieve liberation (*Nirvana*). The opposite of death is birth, both of which are part of this life as we commonly know it. The alternative to this process is liberation, or enlightenment, which the Buddha achieved and which he taught was open to all of us, and which is a state of perfect freedom and total fulfilment. It is known by many names apart from *Nirvana*: The Pure Land, Union with Reality, The Deathless State, Freedom from all Suffering, The Unconditioned, The Unformed, and so on.

In brief, one could say that in many religions the soul has a beginning at or about birth and an everlasting fate depending on this one life. In Buddhism there is no known beginning to our lives, and the origin is lost in the mists of time. But the ultimate fate of each of us can be determined by ourselves, although we are all influenced by each other and our environment also. In theistic religions the soul can hope for a vision of the Divine, whereas in Buddhism the changing person can become a Buddha, an Enlightened One (which is the meaning of the word). For most of us there is some way to go, and possibly many lifetimes of effort, but the goal is there and the achievement of the Buddha testifies to its possibility of realisation.

Death being a stage on our path, it is not viewed with quite the fear that must attach to it in cases where people think that this is the only life, that we live but once, and that death is the end. Nor do Buddhists feel the somewhat frantic haste to 'save their souls', since we see our lives against the large background of eternity, and we understand, however dimly at times, that we are essentially Buddhas.

Between us and this realisation stand the three obstructions of greed, anger and the illusion of a separate and permanent self, and it is the elimination of these three evils that is our proper concern, and the business of Buddhist endeavour.

Peace to all beings!

The Funeral Service

At a funeral, the coffin is brought in to the crematorium chapel and a photograph of the deceased is placed upon or beside the coffin to remind the congregation of the transient nature of life.

A monk who has been invited to conduct the funeral service leads the congregation of Buddhists in the traditional dedications of respect for their Teacher. These are recited in Pāli, the ancient language of Buddhist scripture, each section being repeated three times:

> Exaltation to the Blessed One, saint and perfectly Enlightened One.
> I go for refuge to the Buddha.
> I go for refuge to the Dhamma (his Teaching).
> I go for refuge to the Sangha (the order of Enlightened Disciples).

Next the congregation repeats to the monk the Five Precepts – guidelines and commitments to the moral life. These are voluntary and undertaken freely by each individual as a code of inner spiritual development as well as of action:

> I undertake to maintain the Precept to abstain from harming life.
> I undertake to maintain the Precept to abstain from taking what is not given.
> I undertake to maintain the Precept to abstain from sensual impropriety.
> I undertake to maintain the Precept to abstain from unskilful speech
> I undertake to maintain the Precept to abstain from taking intoxicants which cause heedlessness.

The monk recites a verse in canonical language which bears the following meaning:

> All conditioned things are transient;
> Their nature is to arise and to pass away;
> They are born and they die;
> The cessation of conditioned things is liberation.

To symbolise the transference of pure thoughts (merits) to the departed, the next of kin or a friend pours water from a vessel to an empty bowl until it overflows into a dish below, while reciting the following lines:

> Let the pure thoughts of goodwill be shared by my relative
> and may he (she) be happy.
> As water runs from rivers to fill the ocean,
> So may well-being and merit within us
> Pour forth and reach our beloved departed one,
> Who may thus be filled therewith,
> And share these thoughts with us.

There follows then a sermon on the subject of impermanence. The purpose of the sermon is to bring the mourners to a calm and mature understanding of the universal phenomenon of death, and to realise this in sympathy together. At this time, it is told how the Buddha dealt with the grief of the young mother, Kisāgetami, when she visited him, distraught at the death of her two-year old son who had suddenly been struck down as he played. Taking the corpse of the boy upon her hip, Kisāgetami went, crazed with sorrow, from door to door, saying, 'Give me medicine for my son.'

And people said with contempt, 'Medicine? What is the use? You are mad.' But she understood them not, and walked on till she came to the Buddha.

'Exalted One,' she said, 'Give me medicine for my child, that he may become well again.'

And the Buddha, seeing her condition, said, 'Go enter the town and at any house where yet no one has died, thence bring me some mustard seed.'

'It is well, Lord,' she said, and hurried away on her quest.

Wherever she went the people were ready to give her as much mustard seed as she wanted, but when she told them of the condition laid down by the Buddha, no one could help her, for death had been everywhere at some time or other and taken his toll. And even as the Master had foreseen, Kisāgetami realised the inevitability of death and, taking her child to the grave-yard, had the funeral ceremonies performed, saying aloud that all may hear:

> No village law is this, no city law,
> No law for this clan alone, no law for that one.
> For the whole world, aye, and the gods in high heaven,
> This is the law – all is impermanent, all must die.

CHRISTIANITY

The Catholic Tradition

Liturgy and Belief

The ancient plainsong Requiem Mass was one of the most beautiful pieces in that rich musical tradition. It was also rather sombre. Though the text contained words of hope, rest and peace, the cadences of the music expressed a mood of sorrow which accorded with the black vestments worn. The sequence of the Mass, 'Dies irae, dies illa' added the note of fear. Death was linked to the day of judgement, a 'day of calamity and misery'. The emphasis was on the severity of God's judgement and the narrowness of the way of salvation.

Since the Second Vatican Council, the emphasis has changed. A funeral Mass is now more commonly celebrated in white vestments. Its theme is the resurrection of Christ and its emphasis is not on fear, grief and loss but rather on God's faithfulness to his word and on Christian hope; though it retains a solemnity which reflects the awe which all human beings rightly feel in the face of the dark mystery of death. This change reflects a re-centring of Catholic theology on the resurrection, a return to a view of death, after-life and judgement which is more substantially rooted in the Holy Scriptures. At the same time Catholics also believe tradition, the developing expression of the Church's faith in the course of its history, to be a source of revelation; they also hold to the 'magisterium', the infallibility of the authoritative teaching of the Church's pastors. They also accept the principle 'lex orandi, lex credendi', 'the law of praying is the law of believing'. Doctrinal statements are one language of faith, liturgical practice another. So there can be no disowning of the teaching and practice of the past, where this is in the mainstream of development. The understanding of death and resurrection is necessarily complex.

Sacrament

A doctrinal principle central to Catholic theology is that of sacrament. God's grace in human history is embodied and available in persons and communities. Christ is the first sacrament. Continuing his mission the Church is also an outward sign of inward grace. The Church's seven sacraments bring crucial aspects of human life within the orbit of redemption. One of these sacraments bears directly on sickness and death. It used to be called Extreme Unction. Now it is called more simply The Anointing of the Sick. In the course of it, the priest anoints the forehead and hands of the sick person, saying:

> Through this holy anointing may the Lord in his love and mercy help you with the grace of the Holy Spirit.
> May the Lord who freed you from sin save you and raise you up.

The liturgy puts great emphasis on the body and on the unity of the human person. At funerals too the body is reverenced with incense and with holy water. Some doctrinal statements and some devotional traditions make great use of the language of the separate and disembodied soul, but the liturgy always stresses the unity of body and spirit and looks forward to the resurrection on those terms. The resurrection of the body is not thought of as the gathering up of biological molecules. It is the mysterious re-constitution of the whole person, body and soul, through that power which raised Christ, 'the firstfruits of those who sleep.'

The sacrament of anointing, though a sacrament of healing, looks forward, through sickness towards death. The last Communion received is known as the 'Viaticum', 'food for a journey'. In the commendation of the dying the priest says:

> In the name of God, the almighty Father who created you,
> In the name of Jesus Christ son of the living God who suffered for you,
> In the name of the Holy Spirit who was poured out upon you,
> Go forth, faithful Christian.
> May you live in peace this day,
> may your home be with God in Zion.

The ancient profession of faith, 'Jesus is Lord,' affirmed first of all that Jesus is Lord of death. Death is the most invincible power in the world. All human beings and human institutions lie in its power. Jesus has mastered it and in his kingdom death has no dominion. Christians who inherit new life from him are freed from death's power. Fullness of life is his gift. Hence, although death is so radical an event, there is something illusory about it. It is a transition not a terminus. So the Mass for the Dead prays:

For your faithful Lord
life is changed not taken away.

Hence, although the dead await the resurrection, they do personally await it, continuing to live in the light of God's presence. The character of this survival is mainly a matter for speculation, though theologians like Karl Rahner have developed substantial theories about it (*On the Theology of Death*). Catholic teaching is that the life of the dead continues but is already judged. There is the possibility of damnation, and the possibility of unconditional salvation for those whose wills are perfectly set towards God or totally turned against him. Death marks the end of our personal time in which we make ourselves. But many Christians seem to die with their lives spiritually unfinished. To account for this Catholics pray for the dead and accept the doctrine of purgation after death.

Purgatory

We are all aware of living and no doubt dying full of personal and spiritual imperfections; still with an ingrained egoism which makes us unready for the vision of God. Catholic teaching is that after death the soul is purified by some form of suffering. Purgatory is not a place of punishment. It is a process through which the human will is by prayer and patience purified so as to make heaven possible. The nature of this process is mysterious. It has been vividly imagined by Dante in the *Purgatorio* and again by Newman in *The Dream of Gerontius*. But these are works of the imagination. Doctrinally, we can say that the process involves suffering which is consequent on our own imperfection and evildoing; and that it is progressive, enabling us eventually to live in God's presence.

So the dead are not beyond the reach of our prayers. The doctrine of the Communion of Saints asserts the solidarity of all Christians, those who are still living and striving and 'those who sleep'. There is a community of life through which we suffer from each others' sins and also contribute to the work of each others' redemption. Hence Catholics ask for the intercession of Mary and the saints and also pray for the souls in purgatory. The feast of All Saints (1st November) celebrates the victory of those to whose holiness we owe so much. It is followed by the feast of All Souls (2nd November) where the whole prayer of the Church is directed towards those who are still in the process of purification. The dead are remembered in every Mass, and Catholics say often the prayer:

> Eternal rest grant unto them, O Lord,
> and let perpetual light shine on them.

'All who sleep'

Catholic teaching about eternal life concerns the ultimate destiny of the baptised and the believing. It is couched in the Christian words and ideas of saving faith and grace, sin and repentance. It makes, however, no judgement about the ultimate state of any individual. That judgement of the mystery of a personal life is for God alone. Nor does it make any judgement about the eternal life of the unbaptised and the unbelieving except that it exists. For a long time this concentration on the Christian economy of redemption led to a certain closed exclusiveness. The principle 'extra ecclesiam nulla salus' (outside the Church, no salvation) was rigorously held. But there was always a belief in 'baptism of desire'. An anonymous desire for baptism might be read into moral idealism and goodness of life, but the impression was that the vast majority of mankind lay outside God's plan of salvation.

More recently, Catholic teaching has shifted to emphasise its connection with the corporate destiny of mankind. Eternal life comes through Christ but not necessarily within the structure of Christian belief and practice. The Church has the task of making God's saving grace explicit, but the work of redemption does not go on only inside its visible frontiers. This broadening of the horizons of Catholic teaching to the whole of human life and development can be seen in the social encyclicals of recent popes. It can also be found in the expressions of faith and in the renewed liturgy of the Church. In the Fourth Eucharistic Prayer, this is briefly and beautifully expressed:

Remember those who have died in the peace of Christ, and all the dead whose faith is known to you alone.

The Final Commendation and Farewell is normally preceded by the Funeral Mass.

Final Commendation and Farewell

EXHORTATION

Standing close to the catafalque, the priest gives the following or similar Exhortation to the people.

'It is our solemn duty to carry out, in the traditional manner of God's faithful people, the burial of this mortal body. As we do so, we call trustfully upon God from whom all creation has life. May he in due time by his power, bring to resurrection with all the saints the body of this our brother (sister), which in its frailty we now bury. May God unite his (her) soul with those of all the saints and faithful departed. May he (she) be given a merciful judgement, so that redeemed from death, freed from punishment, reconciled to the Father, carried in the arms of the Good Shepherd, he (she) may deserve to enter fully into everlasting happiness in the company of the eternal King together with all the saints.' (There follows a period of silent prayer.)

FAREWELL CHANT

The body is sprinkled with holy water, before or after the Farewell Chant. The following or any chant may be used. Or all may say together some prayers for the deceased.

Saints of God, come to his (her) aid.
Come to meet him (her), angels of the Lord.
Welcome his (her) soul.

55

*Present him (her) to God the Most High.

May Christ, who called you, welcome you:
and may the angels bring you into the arms of Abraham.
Welcome his (her) soul:
*Present him (her) to God the Most High.

Lord, grant him (her) everlasting rest:
and let perpetual light shine upon him (her).
*Present him (her) to God the Most High.

PRAYER

The Priest then says the following prayer:
'All-merciful Father,
we commend the soul of this our brother (sister)
into your hands.
We are strengthened by the sure hope
that he (she), together with all who have died in Christ,
will rise again with Christ on the last day.
(*We thank you for all the blessings
with which you endowed this servant of yours
in his (her) life on earth.
They are for us too a token of your love,
and of the blessed union of the saints in Christ.)
Listen, then, Lord, in your mercy to our prayers
that the gates of paradise may be opened to your servant
and that we who are left may console one another with
words of faith
(*until we all meet in Christ
and are with you and our brother (sister) eternally.)'
Through Christ our Lord.
Amen.

ANTIPHONS

As the body is taken from the church, one or more of the following Antiphons may be said, or sung, and psalm verses or
other suitable chants added.

---

* may be omitted at choice

56

1. May the Angels lead you into Paradise,
   the Martyrs welcome you as you draw near
   and lead you into Jerusalem, the heavenly city.

2. May the choir of angels welcome you
   and where Lazarus is poor no longer,
   there may you have eternal rest.

3. I am the resurrection and the life:
   He who believes in me, even if he is dead, shall live:
   and all who live and believe in me, will never die.

PSALM

In the Procession to the place of burial, Psalm 117 may be said or sung.

At The Graveside

BLESSING THE GRAVE

If the grave is to be blessed, this is done as follows before the body is placed in it.
   'Let us pray:
   Lord Jesus Christ,
   by your own three days in the tomb
   you made holy the graves of all who believe in you,
   and by so doing you strengthened the hope of resurrection
   in those whose bodies are subject to decay.
   Grant, we pray you, that your servant
   may rest at peace in this grave
   until that day when you, the resurrection and the life,
   enrich him (her) with life made new.
   May he (she) in the light of your countenance
   behold eternal light in heaven.
   You who live and reign for ever.'
   Amen.
The Priest sprinkles with holy water the grave and body and incenses them, if this is customary, unless the rite of *Final Commendation and Farewell* is about to follow.

57

THE BURIAL

As the body is lowered into the grave, or at any other suitable time, the Priest may say:

'It has pleased Almighty God to call our brother (sister) from this life to Himself. Accordingly we commit his (her) body to the earth whence it came. Since Christ, the first-fruits of the dead, has risen again and will refashion our frail body in the pattern of his glorious risen body, we commend our brother (sister) to the Lord. May he embrace him (her) in his peace and bring his (her) body to life again on the last day.'

BIDDING PRAYER

The whole or part of this Bidding Prayer may follow.

'Let us pray for our brother (sister) to our Lord Jesus Christ who has said "I am the resurrection and the life; he who believes in me, though he die, yet shall he live, and whoever lives and believes in me shall never die." We beg you, Lord, who wept over the dead Lazarus, to wipe away the tears from our eyes.
Lord, hear us.'
Lord, graciously hear us.
'We ask you, Lord, who recalled the dead to life, to grant eternal life to this our brother (sister).
Lord, hear us.'
Lord, graciously hear us.
'We call upon you who promised paradise to the repentant thief, to bring this brother (sister) of ours to heaven.
Lord, hear us.'
Lord, graciously hear us.
'Lead our brother (sister), washed by the waters of baptism and anointed with holy oil, into the company of your saints.
Lord hear us.'
Lord, graciously hear us.
'Bring our brother (sister), nourished by the sacred food of your own Body and Blood, to the banquet of your kingdom.

Lord, hear us.'
Lord, graciously hear us.
'Grant that we who mourn for our brother (sister) may be
consoled by faith and strengthened by the hope of everlast-
ing life.
Lord, hear us.'
Lord, graciously hear us.
All may now say the Lord's Prayer or the Priest may say the
following Prayer:
'Show your mercy, Lord,
to this departed servant of yours.
Since he (she) strove to do your will,
let him (her) not be punished for wrong-doing.
And as he (she) was united in the true faith
with all your faithful people,
let him (her) now by your loving goodness
be united with the angelic throng.
Through Christ our Lord.'
Amen.
'Eternal rest grant to him (her), O Lord.'
And let perpetual light shine upon him (her).

The Protestant Tradition

Now the labourer's task is o'er,
Now the battle day is past;
Now upon the farther shore
Lands the voyager at last:
Father, in thy gracious keeping
Leave we now thy servant sleeping.

This hymn, by J. Ellerton, expresses poetically the Christian
understanding of death, at least within the Protestant tradition.
This present life, as a journey of trial and strife, ends in death,
and our mortal flesh is cast aside that we may take up immortality. There are, however, different understandings and emphases within the Christian tradition regarding what actually
happens at death, and what happens afterwards. To under-

59

stand these it is necessary to understand the historical roots of the contemporary Christian tradition.

The Hebrew background

The Old Testament tradition maintained that there was a clear connection between sin and death because sin had no place in the presence of the perfection of God. It was also clear, however, that God took no pleasure in the death even of the wicked – sin and death were evil and had no place in the ultimate purpose of God which could only be good.

The human spirit was thought of as having its own eternal identity. Therefore death was not regarded as the end, as a final dissolution of living things. Rather, it was seen as a joining of the departed souls in the underworld (Sheol). When a man died, he was gathered to his forefathers and dwelt with them in Sheol which was a vague, meaningless place in which one resided, cut off both from the presence of Jehovah (see Ps. 88:5,6,10–12) and from the land of the living.

Later Old Testament passages speak about life after death in ways more real than existence in Sheol. Isaiah 26:19 and Daniel 12:2 suggest that the righteous dead shall share in the coming deliverance and the unrighteous will live in shame and everlasting contempt.

The New Testament

In the Palestine of Jesus it would seem that all except the Sadducees acknowledged some notion of resurrection beyond death and that at some stage there would be a division between the righteous and the unrighteous who would thereafter endure separate existences (see Mark 12:18–27 and Matt. 25:31–46). Thus there is clear reference to judgement and to the eternal and unquenchable fire (see Mark 9:43 and Matt. 18:8). Some would go to eternal punishment, and the righteous to eternal life (see Matt. 25:46).

Paul wrestled at great length (see 1 Corinthians 15) with the notion of resurrection. For him a number of things were clear:
1. Death was the final enemy that had to be conquered because death was the logical consequence of man's sinfulness.
2. That final enemy had been irrevocably conquered by the death and resurrection of Jesus.

3. As God incorporated himself into man's death by becoming incarnate, so man was incorporated (baptised) into his infinite and eternal life in Jesus' resurrection.

4. The resurrection body was not a vague spirit, nor was it a physical body requiring the earthly body for its housing. But it was a separate and recognisable identity, which he called the 'spiritual body'.

5. Christians were promised that they would share Christ's risen life in the fullness of time.

The Early Church

It is thought that in the early centuries of the Christian era, burial ceremonies were joyful affairs with the relatives of the deceased and his Christian friends dressed in white. The person who had died had been released from his mortal flesh and the trials and tribulations of life, and was now at peace. The following prayer is to be found in the 'Prayer Book' of Serapion, Bishop of Thmuis about the middle of the fourth century:

> O God . . . we beseech thee for the repose and rest of this thy servant; give rest to his soul, his spirit, in green places, in chambers of rest with Abraham and Isaac and Jacob and all thy saints: and raise up his body in the day which thou has ordained, according to thy promises which cannot lie, that thou mayest render to it also the heritage of which it is worthy in thy holy pastures. Remember not his transgressions and sins and cause his going forth to be peaceable and blessed . . .

Later Changes

But as the centuries wore on and Christianity was accepted as the dominant religion in more and more countries in Europe, so the total commitment of the early Christian martyrs was seen to be watered down. As a result, the attitude to death and the hope in the after-life underwent a change. There was no longer the certainty of resurrection – it all depended on God's judgement. The former glad confidence in the love of God gave place to an emphasis on God the just and terrible judge. So burial became an occasion for mourning, and the clothes of the relatives changed from white to black. This emphasis was dogmatised at the Council of Trent (1545–1563). According to the Council, the divide between the perfection of God and the sinfulness of man is so great that we shall all need to be purified after death and this purification will be painful. The only difference between this purification and hell will be the length of time involved. The purification will take place in purgatory. Thus the Protestant and Catholic traditions of the Christian Church divided, the former committed to the notion that God's atonement wrought in Christ was appropriated by belief in him in this life, and the latter committed to the notion that cleansing was required after death even for the saved.

The medieval obsession with death, the dead, and prayers for them partly explains the violent reaction by the Reformation against prayers for the departed and the traditional Protestant dislike of the practice. Thus in the English Prayer Book of 1662, requiem masses and prayers for the dead are not included. The contemporary fear of death with its impending judgement was replaced by a sense of hope in the loving forgiveness of God and the power of Christ's resurrection. The opening sentences of the Burial Service all speak of hope:

I am the resurrection and the life, saith the Lord: he that believeth in me, though he were dead, yet shall he live: and whosoever liveth and believeth in me shall never die. (John 11:25,26)

I know that my redeemer liveth, and that he shall stand at the latter day upon the earth. And though after my skin worms destroy this body, yet in my flesh shall I see God: Whom I shall see for myself, and mine eyes shall behold, and not another. (Job 19:25–27)*

We brought nothing into this world, and it is certain we can carry nothing out. The Lord gave, and the Lord hath taken away; blessed be the name of the Lord. (1 Tim. 6:7; Job 1:21)

---

* This rather obscure passage in which the Hebrew is in places unintelligible is regarded by several modern translators as being set in the context of a law court. The New English Bible renders it as follows:

But in my heart I know that my vindicator lives
and that he will rise last to speak in court;

The biblical passage appointed to be read is from Corinthians 15 identifying our hope for life after death with the resurrection of Christ. The prayers express the hope that the deceased will be raised to eternal life, and that those currently mourning his release from the tribulations of life may one day join him.

The proposed Prayer Book of 1928 recognised that many Anglicans regarded the reactions of the Reformation as too extreme and the 1662 Prayer Book as too single-minded. Hence alternative readings and prayers were included making it possible to tolerate some of the emphases against which the Reformation had reacted. Thus prayer for the dead was included for optional use. Lessons were suggested for use at Requiem Mass.

The Teaching of Jesus

In the synoptic gospels (Matthew, Mark and Luke) three points stand out clearly in Jesus' teaching about death: first, the willingness to endure death for his sake is the supreme test of faith (Luke 14:26); second, death is the fixed limit appointed by God to all earthly pleasures, activities and sufferings; and third, death marks the beginning of the true and eternal life with God which cannot be terminated. Thus, for the Christian, there is no need to be over-anxious about the things of this world, neither is there need to be fearful about the next.

The Kingdom of God

Central to the teaching of Jesus was his preaching about the kingdom of God. The good news of the gospel as Christians understood it was that Jesus proclaimed the fact that God was beginning to bring to its fulfilment his original intention in his creation. The reign of God was inaugurated in the incarnation (Jesus' power over demons is understood as meaning that a decisive assault was being made on them). The miracles were enacted proclamations that the kingdom of God had come, and

---

and I shall discern my witness standing at my side
and see my defending counsel, even God himself,
whom I shall see with my own eyes,
I myself and no other.   (*Ed.*)

as such they called forth the response of repentance and faith (see Luke 10:13 = Matt. 11:21). The parables have frequently been described as parables of the kingdom. The reign of God as inaugurated by Jesus is thought to represent the germination of the seed growing secretly. The ministry and life of Jesus corresponds to sowing time rather than to harvest.

The Kingdom is something which God calls into being. It is not something which men build. It is not a utopia nor a new social order; and it is not a mere disposition in men's hearts. It is an act of God himself; it is his initiative in breaking the power of evil, and its consequence, death.

The Christian is incorporated into the suffering, death and resurrection of Jesus, and is thereby said to be in the kingdom. The sacrament of incorporation is baptism. Within the Protestant tradition there is a spectrum of opinion, with members of the Baptist and Pentecostal churches at one end maintaining the necessity of an adult profession of belief to validate the sacrament, and some Anglicans at the other end affirming the efficaciousness of the sacrament in itself irrespective of the quality of the baptised's belief. Wherever along the spectrum a person might be (with certain exceptions such as the Quakers and the Salvation Army who have no sacraments) insofar as he regards anyone as validly baptised so he regards him as being a member of the mystical body of Christ incorporating all other baptised persons in due time to share Christ's eternal risen life.

The kingdom is one in which God's reign has begun but where his purposes for mankind have not yet been fully accomplished. That will occur at the end of time when all will be revealed. Thus a Christian understands himself as being already in the kingdom while yet paradoxically still journeying towards it. Death is for him the point at which time fuses into eternity and that towards which he has journeyed becomes a reality.

For the Protestant, baptism makes a person an inheritor of the kingdom and all the promises associated with it. Thus death is not something to be feared, neither is the after-life to be regarded with trepidation.

The Protestant Christian's attitude to non-believers is somewhat more open. The culturally-bound nature of any proclamation of the Gospel is recognised, and so are the barriers which such culture-bound presentations can create. Some more rigid

Protestants would maintain that the Holy Spirit can over-ride these barriers and people be enabled to hear in spite of them. Their rigidness in some cases leads them to assert that within the scheme of God's creation there cannot be love without justice, and therefore those who die outside the fold of the redeemed community die possibly even outside the saving grace of God.

Most Protestants take a less rigid view, and affirm that it is always the function of the churches to proclaim the saving acts of God. They recognise that the churches themselves are not free from sin, and where this sin creates a barrier, cultural or otherwise, preventing a person from hearing, God himself has and uses power to over-ride the churches' sin, and calls men and women to himself, even though the churches may not recognise the call, and the people themselves not acknowledge it.

An alternative reading proposed for use at burial services in the Anglican Prayer Book of 1928 is the passage in Revelation 21 which looks poetically and symbolically towards the Holy City of the New Jerusalem. It expresses certainty about the reality of the kingdom, and makes no judgements and lays down no conditions about entry to that kingdom, leaving it all in the faithful hands of a God who is supremely understood through his sacrificial love for his human children. 'I am the Alpha and the Omega, the beginning and the end. I will give unto him that is athirst of the fountain of the water of life freely' (21:6). No rules, no regulations, no conditions. Simply God's free gift to be given as only a God who is supremely and utterly loving knows how and is able to give. Since the full nature of that love is incomprehensible to sinful men and women, and since it is infinitely more compassionate than anything that human beings can imagine, it is utterly safe to leave the departed trustingly in his hands.

Current liturgical practice

Most churches of the Protestant tradition concentrate on the following aspects:
1. We do not know what happens after death.
2. We affirm that a notion of purgatory is inconsistent with belief in the kind of God of which Jesus was the supreme incarnate expression.

65

3. We believe that man lives on, because we take seriously Paul's writing on the resurrection.

4. We entrust the departed into the faithful hands of God.

5. We address ourselves to the needs of the bereaved on the grounds that these are the most urgent and the ones that we can actually do something about.

Since 1 Corinthians 15 appears to be the central biblical reference and the basis of the thinking and attitudes which underlie most Protestant funeral services, extracts from that chapter are given below.

But if it is preached that Christ has been raised from the dead, how can some of you say that there is no resurrection of the dead? If there is no resurrection of the dead, then not even Christ has been raised. And if Christ has not been raised, our preaching is useless and so is your faith. More than that, we are then found to be false witnesses about God, for we have testified about God that he raised Christ from the dead. But he did not raise him if in fact the dead are not raised. For if the dead are not raised, then Christ has not been raised either. And if Christ has not been raised, your faith is futile; you are still in your sins. Then those also who have fallen asleep in Christ are lost. If only for this life we have hope in Christ, we are to be pitied more than all men.

But Christ has indeed been raised from the dead, the firstfruits of those who have fallen asleep. For since death came through a man, the resurrection of the dead comes also through a man. For as in Adam all die, so in Christ all will be made alive. But each in his own turn: Christ, the firstfruits; then, when he comes, those who belong to him. Then the end will come, when he hands over the kingdom to God the Father after he has destroyed all dominion, authority and power. For he must reign until he has put all his enemies under his feet. The last enemy to be destroyed is death. For he 'has put everything under his feet.'[1] Now when it says that 'everything' has been put under him, it is clear that this does not include God himself, who put everything under Christ. When he has done this, then the Son himself will be made subject to him who put everything under him, so that God may be all in all.

Now if there is no resurrection . . . why do we endanger ourselves every hour? I die every day – I mean that, brothers – just as surely as I glory over you in Christ Jesus our Lord. If I fought wild

---

[1] Psalm 8:6

beasts in Ephesus for merely human reasons, what have I gained? If the dead are not raised,

'Let us eat and drink,
for tomorrow we die'.[2]

But someone may ask, 'How are the dead raised? With what kind of body will they come?' How foolish! What you sow does not come to life unless it dies. When you sow, you do not plant the body that will be, but just a seed, perhaps of corn or of something else. But God gives it a body as he has determined, and to each kind of seed he gives its own body. All flesh is not the same: Men have one kind of flesh, animals have another, birds another and fish another. There are also heavenly bodies and there are earthly bodies; but the splendour of the heavenly bodies is one kind, and the splendour of the earthly bodies is another. The sun has one kind of splendour, the moon another and the stars another; and star differs from star in splendour.

So will it be with the resurrection of the dead. The body that is sown is perishable, it is raised imperishable; it is sown in dishonour, it is raised in glory; it is sown in weakness, it is raised in power; it is sown a natural body, it is raised a spiritual body.

If there is a natural body, there is also a spiritual body. So it is written: 'The first man Adam became a living being'; the last Adam, a life-giving spirit. The spiritual did not come first, but the natural, and after that the spiritual. The first man was of the dust of the earth, the second man from heaven. As was the earthly man, so are those who are of the earth; and as is the man from heaven, so also are those who are of heaven. And just as we have borne the likeness of the earthly man so shall we bear the likeness of the man from heaven.

I declare to you, brothers, that flesh and blood cannot inherit the kingdom of God, nor does the perishable inherit the imperishable. Listen, I tell you a mystery: We will not all sleep, but we will all be changed – in a flash, in the twinkling of an eye, at the last trumpet. For the trumpet will sound, the dead will be raised imperishable, and we will be changed. For the perishable must clothe itself with the imperishable, and the mortal with immortality. When the perishable has been clothed with the imperishable, and the mortal with immortality, then the saying that is written will come true: 'Death has been swallowed up in victory.'

'Where, O death, is your victory?
Where, O death, is your sting?'

---

[2] Isaiah 22:13

The sting of death is sin, and the power of sin is the law. But thanks be to God! He gives us the victory through our Lord Jesus Christ.

(1 Cor. 15:12–32, 35–57, N.I.V.)

The Eastern Orthodox Tradition

The Office at the Parting of the Soul From the Body

The Abbot cometh to a monk, or his Father Confessor to a layman, and inquireth if there be any word or deed which hath been forgotten, or baseness, or any wrath against any brother, which hath remained unconfessed, or is unforgiven; he must search all there is, and interrogate the dying man concerning each one.

Then the priest beginneth:

'Blessed is our God always, now, and ever, and unto ages of ages. Amen.

'O Holy God, Holy Mighty, Holy Immortal One, have mercy upon us. (*Thrice*)

'Glory to the Father, and to the Son, and to the Holy Spirit, now, and ever, and unto ages of ages. Amen.

'O all-holy Trinity, have mercy upon us. O Lord, wash away our sins. O Master, pardon our transgressions. O Holy One, visit and heal our infirmities, for thy Name's sake.

'Lord, have mercy. (*Thrice*) Glory . . . now, and ever, . . .

'Our Father, who art in heaven, hallowed be thy Name. Thy kingdom come. Thy will be done on earth, as it is in heaven. Give us this day our daily bread. And forgive us our trespasses, as we forgive those who trespass against us. And lead us not into temptation; but deliver us from the Evil One:

'For thine is the kingdom, and the power, and the glory, of the Father, and of the Son, and of the Holy Spirit, now, and ever, and unto ages of ages. Amen.

'Lord, have mercy. (*Twelve times*)

'O come, let us worship God our King. O come, let us

worship and fall down before Christ, our King and our God.
O come, let us worship and fall down before the Very Christ,
our King and our God.' (*Three reverences*)

Psalm 51

A Canon of Prayer to the All-undefiled Birth-giver of God,
with Theme-Songs (*Irmosi*) in the Sixth Tone, on behalf of a
man whose soul is departing, and who cannot speak.

Canticle I
Theme-Song (*Irmos*). When Israel passed on foot over the
deep, as it had been dry land, and beheld their pursuer
Pharaoh engulfed in the sea, they cried aloud: Let us sing
unto God a song of victory.
Refrain: *O all-holy Birth-giver of God, save us.*
Hymns (*Tropari*). Like drops of rain my evil days and few,
dried up by summer's heat, already gently vanish: O Lady,
save me.
'Through thy tenderness of heart and thy many bounties, by
nature inclined thereto, O Lady, in this dread hour intercede
for me, O Helper Invincible!
'Great terror now imprisoneth my soul, trembling unutter-
able and grievous, when forth from the body it must go:
Comfort thou it, O All-undefiled One.
'Glory to the Father, and to the Son, and to the Holy Spirit.
'O Refuge renowned for the sinful and contrite, make thy
mercy known upon me, O Pure One, and deliver me from
the hands of demons: For many dogs have compassed me
about.
'Now, and ever, and unto ages of ages. Amen.
'Lo, now is the hour for succour, lo, now the hour for thine
intercession; lo, now, the time because of which, day and
night I have bowed down before thee, and prayed fervently
unto thee, O Lady.
'Let us pray to the Lord.
'Lord, have mercy.
'O Master, Lord our God Almighty, who willest that all men
should be saved and should come to a knowledge of the
truth; who desirest not the death of a sinner, but that he
should turn again and be saved: We pray thee and beseech

thee, deliver thou the soul of thy servant, *N.*, from every bond, free it from every curse. For thou art he who delivereth them that are bound, and guideth aright them that are cast down, O Hope of the hopeless. Wherefore, O Master, command that the soul of thy servant, *N.*, may depart in peace, and may rest in thine everlasting mansions with all thy Saints; through thine Only-begotten Son, with whom thou art blessed, together with thine all-holy, and good, and life-giving Spirit, now, and ever, and unto ages of ages. Amen.'

Another prayer for a person who hath suffered long, and is on the point of death:

'O Lord our God, who in thine ineffable wisdom hast created man, fashioning him out of the dust, and adorning him with comeliness and goodness, as an honourable and heavenly acquisition, to the exaltation and magnificence of thy glory and kingdom, that thou mightest bring him into this image and likeness; but forasmuch as he sinned against the command of thy statute, having accepted the image but preserved it not, and because, also, evil shall not be eternal: Thou hast ordained remission unto the same, through thy love toward mankind; and that this destructible bond, which as the God of our fathers thou hadst sanctified by thy divine will, should be dissolved, and that his body should be dissolved from the elements of which it was fashioned, but that his soul should be translated to that place where it shall take up its abode until the final Resurrection. Therefore we pray unto thee, the Father who is from everlasting, and immortal, and unto thine Only-begotten Son, and unto thine all-holy Spirit, that thou wilt deliver *N.* from the body unto repose, entreating, also, forgiveness of thine ineffable goodness if he (she) in any wise, whether of knowledge or in ignorance, hath offended thy goodness, or is under the ban of a priest, or hath embittered his (her) parents, or hath broken a vow, or hath fallen into devilish imaginations and shameful sorceries, through the malice of the crafty demon: Yea, O Master, Lord our God, hearken unto me a sinner and thine unworthy servant in this hour, and deliver thy servant, *N.*, from this intolerable sickness which holdeth him (her) in bitter impotency, and give him (her) rest where the souls of the righteous dwell. For thou art the repose of our souls and of our bodies, and unto thee do we ascribe glory, to the Father, and to the Son, and to the Holy Spirit, now, and ever, and unto ages of ages. Amen.'

The Order for the Burial of the Dead (Laymen)

INTRODUCTION

When an Orthodox layman dies his body is washed, after the custom of Apostolic times (Acts 9:37), out of respect to the dead and a desire that he shall present himself clean before the presence of God in the resurrection. Then the body is clothed in new garments, which symbolise our new garment of incorruption (1 Cor. 15:53). The garments thus used correspond to the calling or rank of the departed. They denote that in the resurrection every man must render an accounting to God of the manner in which he has fulfilled his duty in that state of life to which he was called. Thus a monk is dressed in monastic garb, and wrapped in his mantle, which is cut a little, in order that it may be laid about him in the form of a cross; and his face is covered, to denote that in the earthly life he was estranged from the things of this world.

The Psalter is read over the body of an Orthodox believer until the time is come to bury him. This reading comforts those who are mourning the departed, and inclines them to prayer. Inasmuch as the Psalter is designed chiefly to represent prayers for him who has fallen asleep in the Lord, it is interrupted by a commemoration of the dead, with special prayerful petitions to God wherein the dead person is mentioned by name. It is customary to repeat this after each division of the Psalter, as indicated by the Doxology.

Upon the brow of the dead is placed the chaplet, a strip of material upon which are depicted our Lord Jesus Christ, his holy Mother, and St. John the Baptist; together with the Thrice-Holy (O Holy God, Holy Mighty, Holy Immortal, have mercy upon us). The dead Christian is thus adorned with the wreath like an athlete who, with honour, has left the field of contest; or like a warrior who has won a victory. The figures printed thereon signify that he who has run his earthly career hopes to receive the crown for his deeds solely through the mercy of the Triune God and the mediation of the Mother of our Lord and of his Forerunner.

In the hand of the dead is placed a holy picture (*ikona*) of the Saviour, in token that he has believed in Christ and has surrendered his soul to him; that in life he beheld the Lord by anticipation, and now is gone to see him face to face in blessedness, with the Saints. The body of the dead is covered with a holy pall, in token that, as one who has been a believer and has been sanctified by the Sacraments, he is under the protection of Christ.

At funerals four standard candlesticks are placed at the four sides of the coffin, forming a cross. Those present, both at funerals and at Requiem Services (*Panikhidi*), hold tapers, thereby typifying the light divine wherewith the Christian is enlightened at baptism, and the fervour of his prayers. The taper also serves as an image of the world to come, of the light which knows no setting.

THE ORDER

When an Orthodox believer dieth, his relatives straightway give notice thereof unto the priest, who, when he is come to the house in which the remains of the dead man lie, and hath put on his priestly stole (*epitrakhil*), and hath placed incense in the censer, censeth the body of the dead, and those present; and beginneth as usual:
'Blessed is our God always, now, and ever, and unto ages of ages. Amen.'
And those who stand there begin:
O Holy God, Holy Might, Holy Immortal One, have mercy upon us. (*Thrice*)
Glory to the Father, and to the Son, and to the Holy Spirit, now, and ever, and unto ages of ages. Amen.
O all-holy Trinity, have mercy upon us. O Lord, wash away our sins. O Master, pardon our transgressions. O Holy One, visit and heal our infirmities, for thy Name's sake.
Lord, have mercy. (*Thrice*) Glory . . . now, and ever . . .
Our Father, who art in heaven, hallowed be thy Name. Thy

kingdom come. Thy will be done on earth, as it is in heaven. Give us this day our daily bread. And forgive us our trespasses, as we forgive those who trespass against us. And lead us not into temptation; but deliver us from the Evil One: Priest: 'For thine is the kingdom, and the power, and the glory, of the Father, and of the Son, and of the Holy Spirit, now, and ever, and unto ages of ages. Amen.'

And immediately the following Hymns (*Tropari*), are sung:

With the souls of the righteous dead give rest, O Saviour, to the soul of thy servant, preserving it unto the life of blessedness which is with thee, O thou who lovest mankind.

In the place of thy rest, O Lord, where all thy Saints repose, give rest also to the soul of thy servant; for thou only lovest mankind.

Glory . . .

Thou art the God who descended into Hell, and loosed the bonds of the captives. Do thou give rest also to the soul of thy servant.

Now, and ever, . . .

O Virgin alone Pure and Undefiled, who without seed didst bring forth God, pray thou that his (her) soul may be saved.

Deacon: 'Have mercy upon us, O God, according to thy great mercy, we beseech thee: hearken, and have mercy.'

Choir: *Lord, have mercy.* (*Thrice*)

'Furthermore we pray for the repose of the soul of the servant of God departed this life, *N.*; and that thou wilt pardon all his (her) sins both voluntary and involuntary.

'That the Lord God will establish his (her) soul where the just repose.

'The mercies of God, the kingdom of heaven, and the remission of his (her) sins, we entreat of Christ, our King Immortal and our God.'

Choir: *Grant it, O Lord.*

Deacon: 'Let us pray to the Lord.'

Choir: *Lord, have mercy.*

Exclamation: 'For thou art the Resurrection, and the Life, and the Repose of thy departed servant, *N.*, O Christ our God, and unto thee we ascribe glory, together with thy Father who is from everlasting, and thine all-holy, and good, and life-giving Spirit, now, and ever, and unto ages of ages.

Amen.'

Deacon: 'Wisdom!'

Choir: *More honourable than the Cherubim, and beyond
compare more glorious than the Seraphim, thou who without de-
filement barest God the Word, true Birth-giver of God, we
magnify thee.*

Lord, have mercy. (Thrice)

*Glory to the Father, and to the Son, and to the Holy Spirit, now,
and ever, and unto ages of ages. Amen.*

And straightway the Priest giveth the Benediction.

'May Christ, our true God, who hath dominion over the
living and the dead: through the prayers of his all-holy
Mother; of our righteous and God-bearing Fathers; and of all
his Saints, establish the soul of his servant, *N.*, departed
from us, in his holy mansions, and number him (her) among
the just; and have mercy upon us: Forasmuch as he is good
and loveth mankind.'

(Lessons from I Thess. 4:13–18 and from John 5:24–30.)

'Come, brethren, let us give the last kiss unto the dead, ren-
dering thanks unto God. For he (she) hath vanished from
among his (her) kin, and presseth onward to the grave, and
vexeth himself (herself) no longer concerning vanities, and
concerning the flesh, which suffereth sore distress. Where
are now his (her) kinsfolk and his (her) friends? Lo, we are
parted. Let us beseech the Lord that he will give him (her)
rest.

'What is this parting, O brethren? What is this wailing, what
this weeping at the present hour? Come ye, therefore, let us
kiss him (her) who was but lately with us; for he (she) is committed to the grave; he (she) is covered with a stone; he (she)
taketh up his (her) abode in the gloom; he (she) is interred
among the dead, and now is parted from all his (her) kinsfolk
and his (her) friends. Let us beseech the Lord that he will
give unto him (her) eternal rest.

'Now is life's artful triumph of vanities destroyed. For the
spirit hath vanished from its tabernacle; its clay groweth
black. The vessel is shattered, voiceless, bereft of feeling,
motionless, dead: Committing which unto the grave, let us
beseech the Lord that he will give him (her) eternal rest.

'What is our life like unto? Unto a flower, a vapour, and the

74

dew of the morning, in very truth. Come ye, therefore, let us gaze keenly at the grave. Where is the beauty of the body, and where its youth? Where are the eyes and the fleshly form? Like the grass all have perished, all have been destroyed. Come ye, therefore, let us prostrate ourselves at the feet of Christ with tears.

'A great weeping and wailing, a great sighing and agony, and Hell and destruction is the departure of the soul. This transitory life is a shadow unreal and an illusive dream; the trouble of the life of earth is a phantasy importunate. Let us, then, flee afar from every earthly sin, that we may inherit heavenly things.

'As we gaze on the dead who lieth before us, let us all accept this example of our own last hour. For he (she) vanisheth from earth like the smoke; like a flower he (she) is faded; like the grass he (she) is cut down. Swathed in a coarse garment he (she) is concealed in the earth. As we leave him (her) hidden from sight, let us beseech Christ that he will give unto him (her) eternal rest.

'Draw nigh, ye descendants of Adam, let us gaze upon him (her) who is laid low in the earth, made after our own image, all comeliness stripped off, dissolved in the grave by decay, by worms in darkness consumed, and hidden by the earth. As we leave him (her) hid from sight, let us beseech Christ that he will give unto him (her) eternal rest.

'When the soul from the body is about to be rent with violence by Angels dread, it forgetteth all its kinsfolk and acquaintance, and is troubled concerning its appearance before the judgement which shall come upon the things of vanity and much-toiling flesh. Come ye, then, importuning the Judge let us implore that the Lord will pardon him (her) all his (her) deeds which he (she) hath done.

'Come, O brethren, let us gaze into the grave upon the dust and ashes from which we are made. Whither go we now? What are we become? Who is poor, who rich? Who is the master? Who a freeman? Are not we all ashes? The beauty of the countenance is mouldered, and Death hath withered up all the flower of youth.

'Vanity and corruption of a truth, are all the illusions, the inglorious things of life. For all we shall pass away: all we shall die, kings and princes, judges and rulers, rich and poor, and every mortal creature. For now they who were erst alive are cast down into the grave. Wherefore, let us beseech the Lord that he will give rest.

'Now are all the bodily organs seen to be idle, which so little while ago were filled with motion; all useless, dead, unconscious. For the eyes have withdrawn inward, the feet are bound, the hands lie helpless, and the ears withal; the tongue is imprisoned in silence, committed to the tomb. Of a verity, all mortal things are vanity.'

HYMN TO THE BIRTH-GIVER OF GOD

'O thou who savest those who fix their hope on thee, the Mother of the Sun that knoweth no setting, O Progenetrix of God; With thy prayers entreat, we beseech thee, the God exceeding good, that unto him (her) who hath now been translated he will give repose where the souls of the righteous rest. Manifest him (her) an heir of good things divine, in the Courts of the Just, unto everlasting memory, O All-undefiled One.

'As ye behold me lie before you all speechless and bereft of breath, weep for me, O friends and brethren, O kinsfolk and acquaintance. For but yesterday I talked with you, and suddenly there came upon me the dread hour of death. But come, all ye who loved me, and kiss me with the last kiss. For nevermore shall I walk or talk with you. For I go hence unto the Judge with whom is no respect of persons. For slave and master stand together before him, king and warrior, the rich and the poor, in honour equal. For according to his deeds shall every man receive glory or be put to shame. But I beg and implore you all, that ye will pray without ceasing unto Christ-God, that I be not doomed according to my sins, unto a place of torment; but that he will appoint unto me a place where is the light of life.

'Now, and ever, and unto ages of ages. Amen.

'Through the prayers of her who gave thee birth, O Christ; and of thy Forerunner; of the Apostles, Prophets, Hierarchs, Holy Ones, of the Just, and of all the Saints: Give rest unto thy servant who is fallen asleep.'

BENEDICTION

'May he who rose again from the dead, Christ our true God; through the prayers of his all-pure Mother; of the holy, glorious and all-laudable Apostles; of our holy and God-bearing Fathers, and of all the Saints, establish in the mansions of the righteous the soul of his servant, *N.*, who hath been taken from us; give him (her) rest in Abraham's bosom, and number him (her) with the Just; and have mercy upon us, forasmuch as he is good and loveth mankind. Amen.

'Eternal be thy memory, O our brother, who art worthy to be deemed happy and ever-memorable.'

Then straightway the bishop, if one be present, or the priest, reciteth, aloud, the Parting Prayer:

'May the Lord Jesus Christ our God, who gave his divine commands to his holy Disciples and Apostles, that they should bind and loose the sins of the fallen (we, in turn, having received from them the right to do the same) pardon thee, O spiritual child, all thy deeds done amiss in this life, both voluntary and involuntary: Now, and ever, and unto ages of ages. Amen.'

But in place of this prayer, the following, called the Prayer of Absolution, is now generally read, and being printed separately, when the priest hath finished it, he layeth it in the dead person's hand:

'Our Lord Jesus Christ, by his divine grace, as also by the gift and power vouchsafed unto his holy Disciples and Apostles, that they should bind and loose the sins of men: (For he said unto them: Receive ye the Holy Spirit: Whosesoever sins ye remit, they are remitted; and whosesoever sins ye retain they are retained. And whatsoever ye shall bind or loose upon earth shall be bound or loosed also in heaven.) By that same power, also, transmitted unto us from them this my spiritual child, *N.*, is absolved, through me, unworthy though I be, from all things wherein, as mortal, he (she) hath sinned against God, whether in word, or deed, or thought, and with all his (her) senses, whether voluntarily or involuntarily; whether wittingly or through ignorance. If he (she) be under the ban or excommunication of a Bishop, or of a Priest; or hath incurred the curse of his (her) father or mother; or hath fallen under his (her) own curse; or hath sinned by any oath; or hath been bound, as man, by any sins whatsoever, but hath repented him (her) thereof, with contrition of heart: he (she) is now absolved from all those faults and bonds. May all those things which have proceeded from the weakness of his (her) mortal nature be consigned to oblivion, and be remitted unto him (her): Through His loving-kindness, through the prayers of our most holy, and blessed, and glorious Lady, the Mother of our Lord and ever-virgin Mary; of the holy, glorious and all-laudable Apostles, and of all Saints. Amen.'

And the mortal remains are buried with thanksgiving and with joy, and with the song:

'Open, O earth, and receive that which was made from thee.'

Then the body is laid in the grave, and the bishop or the priest, taking a shovelful of dust, streweth it crosswise upon the remains, saying:

'The earth is the Lord's, and the fullness thereof: the round world, and they that dwell therein.'

Then he poureth upon the body oil from the shrine-lamp,[1.] and streweth ashes[2.] from the censer upon it. And thereafter the grave is filled up in the usual way, while these hymns are sung:

With the souls of the righteous dead, give rest, O Saviour, to the soul of thy servant, preserving it unto the life of blessedness which is with thee, O thou who lovest mankind.

In the place of thy rest, O Lord, where all thy Saints repose, give rest, also, to the soul of thy servant: For thou only lovest mankind.

Glory to the Father, and to the Son, and to the Holy Spirit.

Thou art the God who descended into hell, and loosed the bonds of the captives: Do thou give rest, also to the soul of thy servant.

Now, and ever, and unto ages of ages. Amen.

O Virgin alone Pure and Undefiled, who without seed didst bring forth God, pray thou unto him that his (her) soul may be saved.

[1.] That is to say, if the Sacrament of Holy Unction has been performed upon the deceased during his lifetime, the oil and wine which remained therefrom are poured over his dead body. This anointment is Christ's token, and a seal of confirmation that they who die in Christ have wrought for Christ, in the sanctification of their bodies, and have lived uprightly in this earthly life.

[2.] The ashes typify the same thing as the unconsumed oil – the life which is extinguished on earth, yet acceptable unto God; like the sweet spices of the censer.

HINDUISM

The great majority of Hindu philosophers and mystics believe that the soul is immortal. In the *Kathopanisad*, one of the Hindu sacred scriptures, there is a dialogue between the god of Death, and a boy, Nachiketa, who is the symbol of burning curiosity.

Nachiketa: 'This doubt about a man that has gone forth (or died). "He exists," say some. "He exists not," say others. And knowledge of this, taught by thee – this is the third of my wishes.'

Death: 'Even the gods of old were uncertain about this. Not easily knowable, and subtle is this law. Choose, Nachiketa, another wish. Hold me not to it, but spare me this. Choose sons and grandsons of a hundred years, and many cattle and elephants and gold and horses. Choose wealth and length of days. Ask me not of death.'

Nachiketa: 'Tomorrow these fleeting things wear out the vigour of a mortal's powers. Even the whole of life is short. Not by wealth can a man be satisfied. Shall we choose wealth if we have seen thee? Shall we desire life while thou art master? O Death, what is in the great beyond? Tell me of that – this wish that draws near to the mystery. Nachiketa chooses no other wish than that.'

Death: 'Thou indeed, pondering on dear and dearly loved desires, O Nachiketa, hast passed them by. Not this way of wealth hast thou chosen, in which many men sink. Thou art steadfast in the truth – may all like thee, Nachiketa, come to us.

'This soul, the Self, the Atman, is never born and never dies, nor is it from anywhere, nor did it become anything – unborn, eternal, immemorial. This ancient being is not slain when the body is slain; it is smaller than small, greater than great. The Self is hidden in the heart of every being. Understand this great Self – bodiless in bodies, stable in the unstable; the wise man cannot grieve. He has been released from the mouth of death, having gained the one lasting thing above the grave – which is neither sound, nor touch, nor form, nor change, nor taste, nor smell, but is eternal, beginningless, and endless.

'Know that the Self is the rider, and the body the chariot. That the intellect is the charioteer and the mind the reins. The senses, say the wise, are the horses. The roads they travel are the mazes of desire. The wise call the self the enjoyer, when he is united with the body, the senses and the mind.

'As the rain falling on a hill streams down its side, so runs he after many births who sees manifoldness in the Self.

'Like fire, the One takes the shape of every object which it consumes, so the Self, though One, takes the shape of every object in which it dwells.' (*Kathopanisad*)

'As a wagon, heavy laden, might go halting and creaking, so the embodied soul goes halting, over-burdened by the soul of inspiration. When it has gone so far then that man casts aside the body. Just as a caterpillar, when it comes to the end of a leaf, reaching forth to another foothold, draws itself over to it, so the soul, leaving the body and putting off un-wisdom, reaching another foothold there, draws itself over to it.

'As a worker in gold, taking an ornament, moulds it to another form newer and fairer, so in truth the soul, leaving the body here and putting off un-wisdom, makes for itself another form newer and fairer.' (*Brihadavangaka Upanisad*)

Whereas according to some scholars it was inconceivable for the Hebrew to think of a soul without a body, for a Hindu this presents no problem. The body is merely a garment.

'As a man leaves an old garment and puts on one that is new, the spirit leaves his mortal body, and wanders on to one that is new.'

'Weapons cannot hurt the spirit, and fire can never burn him. Untouched is he by drenching waters. Untouched is he by parching winds.'

'Invisible before birth are all beings, and after death invisible again. They are seen between two unseens – why in this truth find sorrow?' (*Bhagavad Gita* ch. 2)

There was a great god-sage called Narada who travelled everywhere, and one day he was passing through a forest and

saw a man who had been sitting meditating until the white
ants had built a huge mound round his body, so long had he
been sitting in that position. And he said to Narada, 'Where
are you going?'

Narada replied, 'I am going to Heaven.'

'Then ask the God of Heaven when he will be merciful to me.
When shall I attain freedom?' said the man. (Freedom means
freedom from the cycle of birth and death.)

Further on Narada saw another man. He was singing and
dancing, and he said, 'O Narada, where are you going?'

Narada replied, 'I am going to Heaven.'

'Then please ask when I shall attain freedom,' said the man.

So Narada went on his way, and in the course of time he came
again along the same road, and he saw again the man who had
been meditating until the ants had built ant hills round him.

'O Narada,' said the man, 'Did you ask about me?'

'Oh yes,' replied Narada.

'What did he say?' said the man.

'He told me that you would attain freedom in four more
births,' replied Narada.

Then the man began to weep and wail and said, 'I have been
meditating until the ant hills have been raised round me, and
I have to endure four more births yet.'

Narada went on, and eventually came to the other man,
who asked,

'Did you ask about me?'

'Oh, yes,' said Narada. 'Do you see this tamarind tree? I
have to tell you that as many leaves as there are on that tree so
many times you will be born, and then you will attain
freedom.'

Then the man began to dance for joy, and said, 'After so
short a time I shall be free!'

And a voice came, 'My child, you shall have freedom this
instant.' (*Kurma Purana*)

This story shows that eagerness to become immortal does not
make one immortal, but to live life meaningfully and joyfully is
the real source of realising immortality.

'The deluded do not see the spirit when it leaves the remains
in the body, nor when moved by the qualities it has experienced

in the world, but those who have the eye of wisdom perceive it, and devotees who industriously strive to do so, see it dwelling in their own hearts.

'The spark of my eternal spirit becomes in this world a living soul, and thus draws around its centre the five senses, and the mind resting in their centre. When the Lord of the body arrives, when he departs, and wanders on, he takes them over with him, as the wind takes perfumes from their places of sleep. When he departs or when he stays, and with the powers of his nature in this life, those in delusion see him not, but he who has the eye of wisdom sees.' (*Bhagavad Gita* ch. 15)

The Viennese psychiatrist, Viktor Frankl has said, 'Man is neither dominated by the will-to-pleasure, nor the will-to-power, but by what he would like to call the "will-to-meaning" – man's deep-seated striving for a higher meaning to existence' (*From Death Camp to Existentialism*). But meaning and purpose can be found only in a universe of unbroken continuity where birth is not a beginning and death is not an end.

In India, the life of man is held to be a pilgrimage not only from the cradle to the grave but also through that vast period of time embracing millions upon millions of years stretching from the beginning to the end of a cycle of evolution (kalpa). Man is held to be a spiritual being, the continuity of whose existence is unbroken. Nations and civilisations rise, grow old, decline and disappear, but the being lives on, spectator of all the innumerable changes of environment. Starting from the great ALL, radiating like a spark from the central fire, he gathers experience in all ages, under all rulers, civilisations and customs, ever engaged in a pilgrimage to the shrine from which he came. To symbolise this, the whole of India is dotted with sacred shrines, to which pilgrimages are made.

Mahatma Gandhi's letter to a disciple, Madeleine Slade, is interesting. The disciple was the daughter of a distinguished admiral, and she relinquished position and comfort to follow Gandhi. He wrote to her:

The more I observe and study things, the more convinced I become that sorrow over separation and death is perhaps the greatest delusion. To realise that it is a delusion is to become free. There is no death, no separation, of the substance, and yet the tragedy of it is that though we love friends for the substance we recognise in them, we deplore the destruction of the insubstantial that covers the substance for the time being. Whereas really friendship should be used to reach the whole through the fragment. You seem to have got the truth for the moment – let it abide for ever. What you say about rebirth is sound. It is nature's kindness that we do not remember past births. Where is the good of knowing in detail all the numberless births we have gone through? Life would be a burden if we carried such a tremendous load of memories. The wise man deliberately forgets many things, even as a lawyer forgets the cases and the details as soon as they are disposed of. Yes, death is but a sleep and a forgetting. Both birth and death are great mysteries. If death is not a prelude to another life, the intermediate period is but a cruel mockery.

In the Hindu view, spirit no more depends on the body it inhabits than the body depends on the clothes it wears, or the house it lives in. When we outgrow a suit, or find our house too cramped, we exchange these for roomier ones that offer our bodies free-er play. Souls do the same. This process by which the individual jiva passes through a sequence of bodies is known as re-incarnation, or transmigration of the soul, in Sanskrit *samskara*. On the human level, the passage is through a series of increasingly complex bodies until at last a human one is attained. Up to this point the soul's growth is virtually automatic. It is as if the soul were growing as steadily and as normally as a plant, and receiving at each successive embodiment a body which, being more complex, provides the needed largesse for its new attainments. With the soul's graduation into a human body, this automatic escalator mode of ascent comes to an end. Its assignment to this exalted habitation is evidence that the soul has reached self-consciousness, and with this estate comes freedom, responsibility and effort. The mechanism that ties these new acquisitions together is the Law of Karma. Karma means roughly the moral Law of Cause and Effect. Every visible event, we are inclined to believe, has its cause, and every cause has its determinative effects.

India extends this concept of universal causation to include man's moral and spiritual life as well. The present condition of each individual's interior life – how happy he is, how confused, or how much he can see – is an exact product of what he has wanted, and got, in the past, and equally his present thoughts and decisions are determining his future status. Each act he directs upon the world has its equal and opposite reaction on himself. Each thought and deed delivers an unseen chisel blow towards the sculpture of his destiny.

'This idea of Karma and the completely moral universe it implies commits the Hindu who understands it to complete personal responsibility. Most persons are unwilling to admit this. They prefer, as the psychologist would say to "project", to locate the source of their difficulties outside themselves. This, say the Hindus, is simply immature' (Huston Smith, quoted in J. Head (comp.), *Re-Incarnation in the World Religions*).

'For beings a human birth is hard to win; then manhood and holiness; then excellence and the path of wise law. Hardest of all to win is wisdom – discernment between Self and not-Self. True judgment, nearness to the Self of the Eternal, and freedom, are not gained without a myriad of right acts in a hundred births.

'The food-form vesture of the body, which comes into being through food, which lives by food, which perishes without food, this form of cuticle, skin, flesh, blood, bone and water – this is not worthy to be the Self, the eternal pure, the Self before birth or death. How can it be born for the moment, fleeting, unstable of nature, not unified, inert, upheld like a jar? For the Self is the witness of all changes of form, the body has hands and feet but not the Self. Though bodiless, yet because it is the Life, because it has power, it is indestructible, it is the Controller, and not the controlled' (*The Crest Jewel of Wisdom*).

To live is by universal consent to travel a rough road; and how can a rough road which leads nowhere be worth the travelling? Mere living – what a profitless purpose! And mere painful living – what an absurdity! There is then nothing to be hoped for, nothing to be expected, and nothing to be done, save to wait our turn to mount the scaffold and bid farewell to that colossal blunder, that much-ado-about-nothing world!

From a Hindu point of view, the wretchedness of human life is not owing to divine punishment, or to original sin, but to ignorance. Not any and every kind of ignorance, but only ignorance of the true nature of Spirit – the ignorance that makes us confuse Spirit with our psychomental experience, that makes us attribute 'qualities' or 'gunas' and predicates to the eternal and autonomous principle that is Spirit. In short, a metaphysical ignorance. It is no wonder that a scholar like Mircea Eliade, in the foreword to his book *Yoga, Immortality and Freedom* says: 'The great discoveries of Indian thought will in the end be recognised. It is impossible, for example, to disregard one of India's greatest discoveries, that of consciousness as a witness, of consciousness freed from its psycho-physiological structures and their temporal conditioning, the consciousness of the liberated man who has succeeded in emancipating himself from temporality and thereafter knows the true inexpressible freedom. This concept of the west, that man is essentially a temporal and historical being, that he can only be what history has made him' is not acceptable to Indian philosophers. In India, through the technique of yoga, it has been possible to go beyond the state of consciousness which is beyond temporality and conditioning.

The Ceremony

In the last stage of life when attachment to this world and its objects has disappeared, the elderly man spends his days in praying. He seriously thinks of the next life after his death. He awaits the appointed time rejoicing in the things of the spirit. He abstains from sensual pleasures and tries to lead his life in a calm and detached way.

After a death contact with the dead body is avoided as far as possible. According to the Sacred Law, the mourners must not have any contact with outsiders lest they carry pollution. They have to restrict themselves to the rigid dietary instructions. They are required to sleep on the floor and must not have their hair cut, nor worship in a temple.

The final ceremony, the *Antyeshti Samskara* is the last of the sixteen purificatory rites. The dead body, all covered in a coffin, is tied on a funeral pyre which is carried on shoulders by the six mourners to the crematorium called the *Shmashana* immediately after the important members of the family have arrived. The eldest of the family leads the mourners who recite

86

all the time, 'Only God's name is true, all else is perishable.' At the burning ground or the crematorium the dead body is put on the heap of firewood. The prayer is recited more or less as contained in the hymns and verses:

'Thou art the Primal God, Ancient Being; Thou art the Final Resting Place of this Universe; Thou art the Knower, the Knowledge and the Supreme Abode; by Thee is the Universe pervaded, and Thy form is infinite.'

'When one layeth his worn-out robes away and takes new ones, so the spirit casts away the old body and takes a new one.'

'Never the Spirit was born, the Spirit shall cease to be never; never was any time when it was not; end and beginning are dreams! Birthless and deathless and changeless remaineth the Spirit for ever; death hath not touched it at all, dead though its body may seem!'

'This no weapons cut, this no fire burns, this no waters wet, and this no wind doth dry.'

'For certain is the death of the born, and certain is the birth of the dead; therefore grieve not for what is inevitable.'

The Gita

'I know the Supreme Absolute Being who is full of splendour like the sun far beyond the darkness of ignorance. By knowing Him alone can one conquer death and attain eternal bliss. There is no other path for the attainment of Salvation.'

Yajur Veda

Now the funeral pyre is lit and the dead body is cremated to the accompaniment of the sacred texts recited by the priest, such as:

'May your eyesight return to the sun, your breath to the winds; may your water mingle with the ocean and your earthly part become one with the earth. The indestructible spirit passes on into another body according to the actions performed in this life.'

Rig Veda

'O Effulgent God! Thou art the Dispenser of Justice; Thou recompensest everyone according to his deeds. Peace be to the Spirit of this dead body in the westward direction. May there be peace to this Spirit also in the east, the north and the south and all other directions. Oh All-knowing and All-illuminator God, Thou art the Creator, the Sustainer and the Destroyer of the Universe. Mayest Thou bestow a worthy abode on this soul.'

Atharva Veda

'Oh Mortal, by thy austerity and enlightenment, and by thy good deeds, attain bliss in heaven and join the Company of thy forbears. Be free from all sins and once again may thy Spirit inherit an enlightened body full of lustre. And once again mayest thou come to this world to perform noble deeds.'

Rig Veda

'The Spirit which is immortal is not made of the five elements and cannot perish. This body will be reduced to ashes and dust. Therefore O Mortal, remember Om, and with Him thy past deeds, the deeds you are doing, as by so doing can one attain salvation.'

Isho Upnishad

'Everything perishes with the death of the body. It is only Dharma that is our best friend, which even after death remains with the Spirit. Therefore do not allow Dharma to perish, for perished Dharma brings about our own destruction.'

Manusmriti

'O Supreme Spirit, lead us from untruth to truth; lead us from darkness to light; lead us from death to immortality.'

'Om Shanti, Shanti, Shanti!' (Om Peace, Peace, Peace.)

The mourners go round the burning pyre in an anti-clockwise direction, and then they bathe in the nearest river, tank or lake, and return home, this time led by the youngest.

On the fourth day from death, the charred bones of the dead person are collected and later on, on a suitable day are thrown into a river, preferably the Sacred River Ganga.

In most cases on the eleventh day, in others on the thirteenth from death, libations of water are poured for the dead. The offering of rice-balls (*pinda*) and vessels of milk are made for him. This is the ceremony performed by orthodox mourners, but often not by the educated. The former believe that on death a man's soul becomes a miserable ghost, *preta*, and is not able to pass on to the world of Fathers or a new birth. It is also believed it may do some harm to the living relatives.

After the last *Antyeshti*, the final rite, the soul acquires a subtle body enabling it to continue its journey. It is also helped on its way and is nourished with the rice-balls offered at subsequent *Shraddha*, after-death ceremonies. After the final ceremony the mourners are no longer impure and therefore return to their normal lives.

HUMANISM

Humanists assume that death is the end of personal existence. For personality is seen to disintegrate with the onset of physical disintegration. The onus is on those who believe that personal existence is independent of physical existence to justify their faith.

In the humanist tradition, the Epicureans made a special point of their teaching on death because of the superstitious fears of death then rampant.

> A right understanding that death is nothing to us makes the mortality of life enjoyable not by adding to life an illimitable time, but by taking away the yearning after immortality. For life has no terrors for him who has thoroughly apprehended that there are no terrors for him in ceasing to live. (*To Menoeceus*, 125)

True to his teaching, on his death-bed Epicurus wrote to a friend:

> On this truly happy day of my life, as I am at the point of death, I write this to you. The disease in my bladder and stomach are pursuing their course, lacking nothing of their natural severity; but against all this is the joy in my heart at the recollection of my conversations with you.

Scattered about the Mediterraean lands during three centuries of dominance before Christ were Epicurean epitaphs: *Non fui, fui, non sum, non curo* (I was not, I have been, I am not, I do not mind). The Epicureans did not celebrate funeral rites. They deprecated and sought to eliminate the craving for immortality in any form (fame, for example) as a source of anxiety and disturbance, unnecessary and destructive of a proper valuation and enjoyment of mortal life, sufficient to those who govern their lives by wise choice and avoidance.

Far from being negative, this attitude is rooted in taking the temporal conditions of all things seriously, as indeed the medium of all existence, the source and condition of all we hold precious. Not to take temporality as seriously as this is in effect contempt of life.

However, an aspiration to an enduring influence as a monument to one's life and work is not the same as this vain craving for immortality. Humanism is creative activity or nothing, and the difference that is made by what anyone does and is need not be recognised and attributed to be real and satisfying. One can be content to remain unknown, the screw under the water, so long as one is at work as a contributing influence to the making of human life, with consequences that persist.

The death of those near and dear is of course a cause of suffering. Bereavement may be one of the hardest blows of fate. The end of an unfulfilled life is especially hard to accept. But neither the tragedy of wasted talent or misspent time nor the triviality of feeble living spoils the picture of what can be and is achieved within the human span of life.

Ceremonies may help the bereaved at this time to take final leave of the physical presence, but respect for the dead asks more than this. The dead are weak, and their claim lies in the hands of those they leave. Like the Epicureans, modern humanists should not make much of funeral rites, disposal of the body, attendance on it at the tomb; rather, they should encourage friends and relatives to come together to contribute from their memories and impressions to the creation of a new image of the person they knew, harvesting what was cultivated and produced in life. In this posthumous context, the dead live on, not immortal but as an influence still at work in the lives they shared. Neglect of the dead was an ancient impiety, and would be not less a modern fault, not the failure to tend a grave, but the lightness that forgets those who have gone as if they had not been.

ISLAM

All that is on earth
Will perish:
But will abide (for ever)
The Face of thy Lord, –
Full of Majesty,
Bounty and Honour. (Qur'an 55:26–27)

Every soul shall have
A taste of death.
And only on the Day
Of Judgment shall you
Be paid your full recompense.
Only he who is saved
Far from the Fire
And admitted to the Garden
Will have attained
The object (of Life):
For the life of this world
Is but goods and chattels
Of deception. (Qur'an 3:185)

It is reported that the Prophet Muhammad during his last illness said: 'Allah, forgive me and have mercy on me and join me to the companion on high (God).' And he said also: 'Allah, help me through the hardship and agony of death.'

Death is the end of the present life but it is not the final end and it is only a temporary separation from the beloved who will all be brought back to life on the day of judgment and, if God wills, be reunited.

When death approaches, a Muslim should be urged to affirm the unity of God by saying the *Kalimat ashshahadah*: (That there is none worthy of worship except God). The dying person should also seek forgiveness and mercy from God. To help the dying person to do so others should read the Qur'an to him.

The chapters of *Ar-Rahman* (55) and *Ya Sin* (36) are always read on such an occasion.

On hearing of a death it is usual to say: 'To God we belong, and to him we return' (Qur'an 2:156).

Relatives and friends gather at the home of the deceased, extend their comfort and solace to the immediate family members, recite the Qur'an and pray that he or she may have God's forgiveness and mercy.

There is a clear rule for washing the body and covering it with a shroud. Great respect should be shown to the dead body. The body is to be washed at least three times with soap or detergent starting with parts of the body as for ablution (for prayer), then wrapped in a special way in three pieces of white cotton cloth. Scent or perfume is also used.

The Prophet Muhammad (peace be upon him) strongly urged Muslims to bury the dead without delay. The body is usually put on a bier or in a coffin, and carried on the shoulders of men to a mosque or direct to the burial ground for the funeral prayer (*salat-ul-Janazah*) which is essential for every dead Muslim. This prayer is a common obligation (*fard kifayah*) on Muslims, and should be said at least by some (though not necessarily by all) of those who are associated with the event after making their ablutions.

The bier (coffin) should be placed in front of the Imam who stands facing *Qiblah* – towards Mecca.

The funeral prayer is offered in congregation and does not include any bowing or prostration. It consists of four *takbirs* (recitation of *Allah Akbar* – God is Most Great). After the first *takbir* praise (*Thana*) is offered and the opening chapter of the Qur'an (*Al-Fatiha*) is read:

Glory to thee, O God, and thine is the Praise, and Blessed is thy Name, and Exalted is thy Majesty and there is none to be served besides Thee.
In the name of God, Most Gracious, Most Merciful.
Praise be to God, the Cherisher and Sustainer of the Worlds; Most Gracious, Most Merciful; Master of the Day of Judgment. Thee do we worship, and thine aid we seek. Show us the straight way, The way of those on whom thou hast bestowed thy Grace, those whose (portion) is not wrath, and

93

who go not astray.

After the second *takbir* the *Ibrahimi* prayer is recited:

O God, exalt Muhammad and the family of Muhammad as thou has exalted Abraham and the family of Abraham, and bless Muhammad and the family of Muhammad as thou has blessed Abraham and the family of Abraham. Thou art the Praised, the Glorious.

Then after the third *takbir* a prayer for forgiveness for the deceased, as follows:

O God, do forgive our living and our dead and our young ones and old ones and our males and our females and those of us who are present and those of us who are absent. O God, he to whom thou hast granted life you have taken from among us, let him die in the faith. O God, do not deprive us of his reward and do not bring us to trial after him.

Then the fourth *takbir* is said followed by *Taslim*:

(Peace be on thee and the mercy of God) by turning the head first right then left.

So the prayer is finished. It is followed by supplication.

The body (on bier or in coffin) is then carried to the burial place. Whenever the procession passes other people on the way, they should stand up to show respect. None shall speak evil of the deceased and all must engage themselves in exalting his virtues and pray for him.

The grave must be excavated deep in order to keep the corpse at a safe depth from the sanitary point of view. The corpse is placed with the face in the direction of Mecca. While this is done the Qur'an is recited, especially the following: 'From the (earth) did We create you, and into it shall We return you, and from it shall We bring you out once again' (Qur'an 20:55).

High grave-stones or monuments are forbidden and were disliked by the Prophet Muhammad (peace be upon him). Graves should be little above ground.

Mourning at death is natural. Grief which arises sincerely from the depth of the heart cannot be prevented. The Prophet (peace be on him) himself wept on the death of his son Ibraham and of some of his beloved companions. Loud wailings followed by striking of breasts, hands and feet, and tearing of clothes is forbidden.

In Muslim countries the mourning period varies from seven days to forty days and even up to three months. During this period no joyful events (such as weddings) may take place. This applies not only to the immediate family of the deceased but to all distant relatives as well.

Graves are a reminder of death and the hereafter. The Prophet (peace be on him) used to say when he visited graves: 'Peace be upon you, O inmates of the graves. You have preceeded us, and we are following.' Visits on Eid days are especially recommended.

Alms may be given on behalf of the dead. The Prophet said: 'When a man dies his actions cease except for three: continuous charity (paid on his behalf), knowledge he leaves behind (for the benefit of the people), and a pious son (or daughter) who prays for him.'

Life in the grave is the period from death to the time of Resurrection when judgment will take place. One person may feel pain in separation from the world while another may feel pleasure. A virtuous person will live in a state of happiness in his grave while the sinner will live in continual agony.

Muslims believe that on the Day of Judgment all the dead will be raised and will be brought to their account before God. Records of their deeds (bad ones and good ones) will be put in front of them. Reward or punishment will be given in impartial justice, with great mercy.

On that Day will men
Proceed in companies sorted out,
To be shown the Deeds
That they (had done).

Then shall anyone who
Has done an atom's weight
Of good, see it!

And anyone who
Has done an atom's weight
Of evil, shall see it. (Qur'an 99:6–8)

The following points are also important:

Post-mortem is forbidden except in very special circumstances.

Prolonging life by artificial methods is forbidden.

Muslims should be buried among Muslims in a Muslim cemetery.

Cremation is absolutely forbidden.

A Muslim should be buried preferably at the place of death. (It is unnecessary to send a body back to the place of birth.)

Selections from the Holy Qur'an concerning the Day of Judgement.

Chapter 88 (The Overwhelming Event)[1]

In the name of God, the Beneficent, the Merciful.

1. Has the story
Reached thee, of
The Overwhelming (Event)?

2. Some faces, that Day,
Will be humiliated,

3. Labouring (hard), weary,

4. The while they enter
The Blazing Fire, –

5. The while they are given,
To drink, of a boiling hot
spring,

6. No food will there be
For them but a bitter Dhari[2]

7. Which will neither nourish
Nor satisfy hunger.

8. (Other) faces that Day
Will be joyful,

9. Pleased with their Striving,

10. In a Garden on high,

11. Where they shall hear
No (word) of vanity:

12. Therein will be
A bubbling spring:

13. Therein will be Thrones
(Of dignity), raised on high.

[1]. See also chapter 30.
[2]. The root-meaning implies again the idea of humiliation. Metaphorically, it is understood to be a plant, bitter and thorny, loathsome in smell and appearance, which will neither give fattening nourishment to the body nor in any way satisfy the burning pangs of hunger – a fit plant for Hell.

96

14. Goblets placed (ready),

15. And Cushions set in rows,

16. And rich carpets
(All) spread out.

17. Do they not look
At the Camels,
How they are made ?–

18. And at the Sky,
How it is raised high?–

19. And at the Mountains,
How they are fixed firm?–

20. And at the Earth,
How it is spread out?

21. Therefore do thou give
Admonition, for thou art
One to admonish.

22. Thou art not one
To manage (men's) affairs.

23. But if any turn away
And reject God, –

24. God will punish him
With a mighty Punishment,

25. For to Us will be
Their Return;

26. Then it will be for Us
To call them to account.

Chapter 84 (The Rending Asunder)

In the name of God, Most Gracious, Most Merciful.

1. When the Sky is
Rent asunder,

2. And hearkens to
(The Command of) its
Lord, –
And it must needs
(Do so);–

3. And when the Earth
Is flattened out,

4. And casts forth
What is within it
And becomes (clean) empty,

5. And hearkens to
(The Command of) its
Lord, –
And it must needs
(Do so); – (then will come
Home the full Reality).

6. O thou man!
Verily thou art ever
Toiling on towards thy
Lord –
Painfully toiling, – but thou
Shalt meet Him.

7. Then he who is given
His Record in his
Right hand,

8. Soon will his account
Be taken by an easy reckoning,

9. And he will turn
To his people, rejoicing!

10. But he who is given
His Record behind his
back, –

11. Soon will he cry
For Perdition,

12. And he will enter
A Blazing Fire.

13. Truly, did he go about
Among his people, rejoic-
ing!

14. Truly, did he think
That he would not
Have to return (to Us)!

15. Nay, nay! for his Lord
Was (ever) watchful of him!

16. So I do call
To witness the ruddy glow
Of Sunset;

17. The Night and its Homing;

18. And the Moon
In her Fulness:

19. Ye shall surely travel
From stage to stage.

20. What then is the matter
With them, that they
Believe not? –

21. And when the Qur'an
Is read to them, they
Fall not prostrate.

22. But on the contrary
The Unbelievers reject (it)

23. But God has full Knowledge
Of what they secrete
(In their breasts)

24. So announce to them
A Penalty Grievous,

25. Except to those who believe
And work righteous deeds:
For them is a Reward
That will never fail.

Chapter 83 (Dealing in Fraud)

In the name of God, Most Gracious, Most Merciful.

1. Woe to those
That deal in fraud, –

2. Those who, when they
Have to receive by measure
From men, exact full
measure,

3. But when they have
To give by measure
Or weight to men,
Give less than due.

4. Do they not think
That they will be called
To account?–

5. On a Mighty Day,

6. A Day when (all) mankind
Will stand before
The Lord of the Worlds?

7. Nay! Surely the Record
Of the Wicked is
(Preserved) in Sijjin.[1]

8. And what will explain
To thee what Sijjin is?

9. (There is) a Register
(Fully) inscribed.

[1]. This is a word from the same root as Sijn, a prison.

10. Woe, that Day, to those
That deny–

11. Those that deny
The Day of Judgment.

12. And none can deny it
But the Transgressor
Beyond bounds,
The Sinner!

13. When Our Signs are
rehearsed
To him, he says,
'Tales of the Ancients!'

14. By no means!
But on their hearts
Is the stain of the (ill)
Which they do!

15. Verily, from (the Light
Of) their Lord, that Day,
Will they be veiled.

16. Further, they will enter
The Fire of Hell.

17. Further, it will be said
To them: 'This is
The (reality) which ye
Rejected as false!'

18. Nay, verily the Record
Of the Righteous is
(Preserved) in 'Illiyun.²

19. And what will explain
To thee what 'Illiyun is?

20. (There is) a Register
(Fully) inscribed,

21. To which bear witness
Those Nearest (to God).

22. Truly the Righteous
Will be in Bliss:

23. On Thrones (of Dignity)
Will they command a sight
(Of all things):

24. Thou wilt recognise
In their Faces
The beaming brightness of
Bliss.

25. Their thirst will be slaked
With Pure Wine sealed:

26. The seal thereof will be
Musk: and for this
Let those aspire,
Who have aspirations:

27. With it will be (given)
A mixture of Tasnim:

28. A spring, from (the waters)
Whereof drink
Those Nearest to God.

29. Those in sin used
To laugh at those
Who believed,

30. And whenever they passed
By them, used to wink
At each other (in mockery):

31. And when they returned
To their own people,
They would return jesting;

32. And whenever they saw
them,
They would say, 'Behold!
These are the people
Truly astray!'

33. But they had not been
Sent as Keepers over them!

34. But on this Day
The Believers will laugh
At the Unbelievers:

². The place where the Register of the Righteous is kept.

35. On Thrones (of Dignity)
They will command (a sight)
(Of all things).

36. Will not the Unbelievers
Have been paid back
For what they did?

Chapter 78 (The Great News)

In the name of God, Most Gracious, Most Merciful.

1. Concerning what
Are they disputing?

2. Concerning the Great News,

3. About which they
Cannot agree.

4. Verily, they shall soon
(Come to) know!

5. Verily, verily they shall
Soon (come to) know!

6. Have We not made
The earth as a wide
Expanse,

7. And the mountains as pegs?

8. And (have We not) created
You in pairs

9. And made your sleep
For rest,

10. And made the night
As a covering,

11. And made the day
As a means of subsistence?

12. And (have We not)
Built over you
The seven firmaments,

13. And placed (therein)
A Light of Splendour?

14. And do We not send down
From the clouds water
In abundance,

15. That We may produce
Therewith corn and vegetables,

16. And gardens of luxurious
growth?

17. Verily the Day
Of Sorting Out
Is a thing appointed, –

18. The Day that the Trumpet
Shall be sounded, and ye
Shall come forth in crowds;

19. And the heavens
Shall be opened
As if there were doors,

20. And the mountains
Shall vanish, as if
They were a mirage.

21. Truly Hell is
As a place of ambush, –

22. For the transgressors
A place of destination:

23. They will dwell therein
For ages.

24. Nothing cool shall they taste
Therein, nor any drink

25. Save a boiling fluid
And a fluid, dark, murky,
Intensely cold, –

26. A fitting recompense
(For them).

27. For that they used not
    To fear any account
    (For their deeds),

28. But they (impudently)
    treated
    Our Signs as false.

29. And all things have We
    Preserved on record.

30. 'So taste ye (the fruits
    Of your deeds);
    For no increase
    Shall We grant you,
    Except in Punishment.'

31. Verily for the Righteous
    There will be
    A fulfilment of
    (The Heart's) desires;

32. Gardens enclosed, and
    Grapevines;

33. Companions of Equal Age;

34. And a Cup full
    (To the Brim).

35. No Vanity shall they hear
    Therein, nor Untruth; –

36. Recompense from thy Lord,
    A Gift, (amply) sufficient,

37. (From) the Lord
    Of the heavens
    And the earth
    And all between, –
    (God) Most Gracious:
    None shall have power
    To argue with Him.

38. The Day that
    The Spirit and the angels
    Will stand forth in ranks,
    None shall speak
    Except any who is
    Permitted by (God) Most
    Gracious,
    And he will say
    What is right.

39. That Day will be
    The sure Reality:
    Therefore, whoso will, let
    him
    Take a (straight) Return
    To his Lord!

40. Verily, We have warned you
    Of a Penalty near, –
    The Day when man will
    See (the Deeds) which
    His hands have sent forth,
    And the Unbeliever will say,
    'Woe unto me! Would that
    I were (mere) dust!'

These extracts from the Qur'an are taken from the translation by Abdallah Yousuf Ali published by the Call of Islam Society (Libyan Arab Republic).

JUDAISM

Rabbi Meir sat in the House of Study and preached one Sabbath afternoon. While he was there, his two sons died. His wife, Beruria, laid them on their beds, and covered them with a linen sheet. After sunset, Rabbi Meir returned, and made the blessings over the outgoing of the Sabbath.

'Meir, I have a question to ask you,' said Beruria. 'Someone came and deposited some precious articles here; today he came and asked for their return – should I give them to him?'

'Of course!' replied Meir.

At that, she took his hand and led him to the room where his sons lay. Meir burst into tears. 'The Lord gives and the Lord taketh away; Blessed be the name of the Lord.'

> (*Midr. Prov.* XXXI, 10)

'Death' as an abstract concept is not a theological 'problem' in Judaism. We see death as part of the destiny of the individual, one stage on a 'Path of Life'.

> Rabbi Jacob said: This world is like a vestibule before the world to come; prepare yourself in the vestibule, so that you may enter the banquet hall. (*Mishnah Avot* 4:21)

Yet Judaism recognises fully the traumatic loss which each death represents to the living community; and Jewish customary law (*Halakhah*) has evolved a hierarchy of mourning patterns which serve to cushion the mourners through the several stages of their grief. In themselves, the patterns of mourning reflect Jewish attitudes to death and the dying.

Judaism traditionally does not begin with the formulation of a philosophy and on that basis proceed to decide upon consequent modes of action . . . The primary Jewish task is to obey God by practising the commandments. The attitudes that inform them will thereby eventually and inevitably become one's own. By living and studying the *Halakhah* one gradually discovers and absorbs the theological and moral sources upon which it is based. The method is inductive rather than deductive. (*The Good Society: Jewish Ethics in Action*, N. Lamm, Viking Press USA)

Preparation for death

When a sick person realises their life is ebbing away, they recite the 'Confession on the death bed' (*viddui*).

This short Hebrew prayer:
acknowledges that cure and death are in the hands of God; asks for healing, but accepts the possibility of death; requests that death should atone for sins committed during life; asks for length of years for the relatives of the dying person; asks that, in the event of death, God should 'convey to me something of the great goodness stored up for the righteous – make known to me the path of everlasting life – for in your presence is complete joy, and happiness is always at your right hand.'

The words of the monotheistic declaration (*She'ma*) 'Hear, Israel, the Lord our God is one God' are the last words of the dying person. A Jewish legend states that the last sigh of a dying man reverberates from one end of the world to the other.

It is forbidden to hasten the death of a dying person under any circumstances; but, in the case of a life which is ending in dignity at its full span, neither need unnecessary steps be taken to prolong life. In other cases, however, every effort must be made to preserve life. Every law, custom or tradition must be disregarded in circumstances when they represent – in even the remotest way – an impediment to the saving of human life.

The Soul

The moment of death is referred to in Jewish sources as the 'Time of the departure of the soul' (*Sha'at yetziat ha-neshamah*). Judaism believes that the soul of a person ascends to a 'World to come' (*Olam Ha'ba*). The soul, (*Nefesh, Neshamah* or *Ruach*) is an integral component of every human being. The soul existed before creation; according to Jewish mystic tradition, they were present at Mount Sinai to witness the revelation; given by God, they return to him at the death of the body.

The daily liturgy states:

My God, the soul which you have placed within me is pure. You have created it; you have formed it; you have breathed it into me. You preserve it within me, you will take it from me, and restore it to me in the hereafter. So long as the soul is within me, I offer thanks before you, Lord my God and God of my fathers, Master of all creatures, Lord of all souls. Blessed are you, O Lord, who restores the souls to the dead.

Death: the community's responsibility

Among the main organisations of every Jewish community is the 'Holy Fraternity' (*Hevra Kadisha*). This is a voluntary group, membership of which is considered an honour and a holy duty, whose task it is to supervise and carry out all rites and arrangements connected with death and burial. The task of dealing with death devolves on the entire community; all work must stop until satisfactory arrangements are made for according the correct dignity to the body of a person who has just died. The members of the *Hevra Kadisha* are responsible for acquiring and maintaining cemeteries; attending to the dead; carrying out funerals and looking after the mourners.

Although many communities still maintain an entirely voluntary *Hevra Kadisha*, nowadays many of its duties are carried out by professionals. However, burial in Jewish cemeteries is always by Burial Societies of the Jewish community – whether honorary or professional – on an entirely non-commercial basis.

Burial

After the 'departure of the soul' the bodily remains must be treated with great respect. The body is not left alone, by day or night, until the funeral. It is invariable Jewish practice that the funeral takes place as soon as possible after death – usually within 24 hours. Before the funeral, the body is thoroughly washed (*Taharah*, literally purification) by the members of the *Hevra Kadisha*. No embalming, preservative, or cosmetic of any sort is permitted to be used on the corpse. It is dressed in simple white garments, and buried in a plain, unembellished and unvarnished wooden coffin. The burial service is short, lasting approximately half-an-hour, and normally includes an eulogy (*Hesped*). It begins with the declaration:

> The Rock, his work is perfect, for all his ways are judgement, a God of faith, without iniquity; just and upright is He . . .

The dominant themes of the Burial service are:
(i)   the recognition of God as the 'True Judge' (*Dayan Emet*)
(ii) the cycle of man's life:

> As for man, his days are as grass, as the flower of the field, so he flourishes. For the wind passes over it and it is gone – it is no longer known in its place.

(iii) an extremely powerful expression of belief in the progress of the soul:

> O Lord, who is full of compassion, who dwells on high, God of forgiveness, who is merciful, slow to anger and abounding in loving kindness, grant pardon of transgressions, nearness of salvation, and perfect rest beneath the shadow of your divine presence, in the exalted places among the holy and pure, who shine as the brightness of the firmament, to . . . who has gone to his/her eternal home. We beseech you, O Lord of compassion, remember unto him/her for good all the meritorious and pious deeds which he/she wrought while on earth. Open unto him/her the gates of righteousness and light, the gates of pity and grace. O shelter him/her for evermore under the cover of your wings; and let his/her soul be bound up in the bond of eternal life. The Lord is his/her eternal inheritance; may he/she rest in peace. And let us say, Amen.

Afterlife

Jewish teaching has always maintained that since no human can possibly know the nature of life after death, speculation on the form it takes is pointless, and is actively discouraged. Yet there is a quite definite belief in the Afterlife, and in reward and punishment. Jewish thinking, generally speaking, does not suggest 'Heaven and Hell'; rather that the righteous will enjoy nearness to God in the world to come, sitting before him and imbibing the Divine Radiance; but the less righteous will have only a more distant experience. Belief in the continuance of life is underlined by the constant use of terms meaning 'life' for concepts associated with death. The cemetery, for example, is known in Judaism as 'the House of Life' (*Bet Hahayyim*). The World to come is a finite period which will end with the End of Days and the Revival of the Dead.

Mourning

Close relatives of the deceased – spouse, parents, children, brothers and sisters – are considered mourners. Comforting of the mourner (*Nihum Avelim*) is considered in Judaism as one of the primary social duties. There are four periods of mourning:

(a) *From death until burial*: During this period the mourner is known as an *Onen*. He/she should spend this time arranging the preparations for the funeral; the *Onanim* (plural) are exempt from certain religious obligations (e.g. regular prayer). During this time the mourner is not comforted: 'Rabbi Simeon ben Elazar said: ". . . do not comfort your fellow while his dead lies before him . . ."' (*Mishnah Avot* 4:23)

At the commencement of the funeral the mourners tear one of their garments – this act of mourning is known as *Kriah* (tearing).

(b) *The Shiva*: For seven days after the funeral, the close relatives gather daily at the house of mourning. They sit on low chairs, and family, friends and neighbours come to offer them comfort and condolence. Daily prayers, including special prayers in memory of the deceased are said. During the period of the *Shiva* (literally seven) deep mourning is observed. The mourners may not shave, have their hair cut, go to work, or prepare food for themselves.

(c) *Shaloshim*: For a further three weeks (until *Shaloshim*, thirty days after the funeral) personal mourning is observed. The mourner may go to work, but should avoid, if possible, shaving and haircuts; no new clothes may be worn, nor may the mourner listen to any music or take part in any celebration.

Mourners have the privilege of reciting a particular piece

of the liturgy – the *Kaddish* (see below) – at all public prayers that they attend. Most Jewish people see the observance of this privilege as a duty – and will make every effort to attend synagogue services during their period of mourning.

(d) *From Shaloshim to first Yahrzeit*: The full period of mourning, observed for parents and children, is one year from the date of death. *Kaddish* is said for eleven months; and during this time the *Avelim* (mourners) still observe certain patterns of mourning. The tombstone may be erected and consecrated at any time from the end of the *Shaloshim*, but not normally later than the first *Yahrzeit* (anniversary of death, from Yiddish). Each year the *Yahrzeit* is marked by reciting *Kaddish*, lighting a memorial candle and performing some righteous act.

Kaddish

This prayer is one of the best known parts of the Jewish liturgy. Although used for different purposes originally, for centuries now, one variant of it, the 'Mourners Kaddish' has been used exclusively for recitation by mourners in the synagogue. It is said in its original language, Aramaic. It is neither a prayer for the dead nor to the dead, but a powerful assertion by a mourner who has encountered death at close quarters of faith in the Creator, ending with a plea for peace.

> Glorified and sanctified be God's great name throughout the world which he has created according to his will. May he establish his kingdom in your lifetime and during your days, and within the life of the entire house of Israel, speedily and soon; and say, *Amen*.
> May his great name be blessed forever and to all eternity.
> Blessed and praised, glorified and exalted, extolled and honoured, adored and lauded be the name of the Holy One, blessed be he, beyond all the blessings and hymns, praises and consolation that are ever spoken in the world; and say, *Amen*.
> May there be abundant peace from heaven, and life, for us and for all Israel; and say, *Amen*.
> He who creates peace in his celestial heights, may he create peace for us and for all Israel; and say, *Amen*.

Note: Described above is traditional Jewish belief and practice, as still observed by the Orthodox Jewish community. The Reform and Liberal Jewish communities have amended the rituals of mourning in a number of ways – for example cremation is permitted, *Shiva* is not necessarily observed for the full seven days; *Kriah* is not observed. However, the basic belief and principles as outlined above are common to all sections of the Jewish community.

The following prayer is used by some Reform Synagogues:

Prayer in the Home Before a Funeral

'Merciful Father, be with us as we gather in this house, the home of our dear one who has gone forward to life everlasting. We remember all his/her goodness. May his/her memory be a blessing.

'Help us to remember that the soul does not die, and our dear one has gone to that eternal home which you prepared for us when our work on earth is done, and our time here has ended. Open the gates of mercy for him/her. May he/she enter into everlasting peace. In your light we see beyond the frontiers of death to the life that has no end.

'This house was built by human hands, but we shall come together in a home where we shall never part, surrounded by Your presence. *Amen.*'

Psalm 23 may then be said.

Memorial Service

(part of a service in the home or in the synagogue)

'The souls of the righteous are in the hands of God, and no harm shall touch them. In the eyes of the ignorant they appeared to die, and their going seemed to be their hurt. But they are at peace, and their hope is full of immortality. Their chastening was slight compared to the great good they shall receive. God has put them to the test and proved them worthy to be with him.

'Lord God, source of all being and fountain of life, what can we say to you, for you see and know all things. In your wisdom you formed the universe and in your love you provide for all your creatures. What can we do, but acknowledge your power, accept your gifts with gratitude, and according to your will, give you back your own.

'Lord God, may the light of your presence shine on us as we gather here, our hearts bowed down by the loss of . . . whom you have gathered to yourself. Accept in your great mercy the earthly life which has now ended and shelter with your tender care this soul that is so precious to our hearts.

'We thank you for all that was gentle and noble in his/her life. Through his/her name inspire us with strength and light. Help us to use our grief itself for acts of service and of love.

'Everlasting God, help us to realise more and more that time and space are not the measure of all things. Though our eyes do not see, teach us to understand that the soul of our dear one is not cut off. Love does not die, and truth is stronger than the grave. Just as our affection and the memory of the good he/she did unite us with him/her at this time, so may our trust in you lift us to the vision of the life that knows no death.

'God of our strength, in our weakness help us; in our sorrow comfort us; in our confusion guide us. Without you our lives are nothing; with you there is fullness of life for evermore.

'May the words of my mouth and the meditation of my heart be acceptable to you, O Lord, my rock and my redeemer.

'God full of compassion whose presence is over us, grant perfect rest beneath the shelter of your presence with the holy and pure on high who shine as the lights of heaven, to . . . who has gone to his/her everlasting home. Master of mercy, cover him/her in the shelter of your wings forever, and bind his/her soul into the gathering of life. It is the Lord who is his/her heritage. May he/she be at peace in his/her place of rest. *Amen.*'

SIKHISM

The Riddle of Birth and Death
In the Sikh scriptures reflections on death are found always associated with birth and the words *janam* (birth) and *maran* (death) generally occur together. This is because the mystery of death cannot be understood without knowing the human and spiritual purpose of birth in this world. Man is given sufficient free will to be responsible for his destiny and fate within the life span of birth and death, but the Unknown before birth and the Unknown after death is God, the Sovereign of both the apparently dark ends of human life (dohān siriān kā swāmī). Before sending us into this world as human beings, God gave us a purpose and direction which was ingrained in our consciousness. Wordsworth rightly talks of the dim recollections of these intimations of immortality which the child, according to Sikh scriptures, vividly remembers in the womb of the mother and during his infancy.

Man is not born in sin as some would have us believe, but he is born in God's grace. Sin only leads to birth and deaths in lower lives of animal existence, while God's grace gives the soul an opportunity to become a god in flesh. Human birth is something which even the angels covet, because it is only as human beings that we can rise to the perfection of the ultimate Being. While the mystery of the Unknown before birth and after death baffles man, God has not left this mystery unveiled. In different ages and in different climes he has sent prophets on this earth who have not only unveiled this mystery and created an unending yearning for immortality but have left divine Wisdom enough to exalt men to a vision which can conquer not only human frailty but also death.

According to the divine revelation and the mystical vision of Guru Nanak, 'What is in the universe is also found in the human body and he who seeks will find it,' and, 'Such is the divine play of the Creator that he has reflected the whole Cosmos in the human body' (*Adi Granth*). It is within an enlightened mind and heart that the Cosmos is evaluated and existence and Being are revealed in the full splendour of divine Majesty. This is the metaphysical basis of the Guru's teachings about death and immortality. It is at the root of this divine certitude that man is in a position constantly to assert that each man can recognise in every other the fact of human transcendence.

> The drop of water is in the sea,
> And the sea is in the drop of water,
> Who shall solve the riddle?
> The Word leads to inner concentration,
> And concentration leads to divine Wisdom,
> This is the riddle of the divine Word.
> The eternal Light dwells in human mind,
> And human mind is the emanation of the Light,
> Our five senses become the disciples of Light.
> (*Sacred Writings of the Sikhs*).

Man is not born free, but he is born to be free. Those who lack spiritual consciousness are helpless victims of their own instincts and wild cravings and they drift away from truth. He who lives the life of contemplation will be blessed with inner illumination. The white man and the black man, the heathen and the negro, the saint and the wicked, the rich and the poor, are all moulded out of the same fundamental elements, and infused with the same divine Spark of Life, and are looked after and sustained by the same God. Religions may differ, but the human elements and the divine elements in man do not differ anywhere or at any time. God, the ultimate Truth is ever the same.

> All men are moulded out of the same clay,
> The Great Potter hath merely varied the shapes of them,
> All men are mixed of the same five elements,
> No one can make any element less in one, more in another.
> Man is born in chains,
> Without meeting the True Guru,
> He cannot attain liberation. (*Sacred Writings*)

Long is the night of life which is spent in egoistic indifference to truth, in reckless ignorance of righteousness, justice and wisdom. Short is the day in which man toils and suffers for

Trust, Beauty and Love. The face of eternal Truth and eternal Life is hid as it were under a golden lid. The purpose of life is to open this lid and visualise this Truth beyond birth and death.

Mortal Man And Immortality

A Yiddish proverb says, 'Everyone knows he must die, but no one believes it.' Man lives in conscious ignorance of death. He can think of life and its urge for immortality but does not stop to think that the silence and darkness of death broods over all. It is death which gives meaning and purpose to life. It is death which makes man think whether he will end up in the grave or be immortal. 'Blessed is he who has always the hour of death before his eyes and everyday disposes himself to die.' People are generally so absorbed in the present attractions of life that they never care to think of death. Death pounces on them, sweeping down on heedless man like a bird of prey.

> Death is at large O Friend,
> Like a blood-thirsty beast,
> Ready to devour any prey:
> Bear it in mind and never forget,
> It will pounce on you some day
> Contemplate the Lord, sayeth Nanak,
> Life's precious years are passing away.
> (Guru Tegh Bahadur, *Padavali*)

Though destined for immortal life, the soul of man is trapped in false belief that the body is his self. Clinging to the perishable things of the world, he shares their fate and is subject to mortality, the victim of his sins and is dragged again and again into physical birth by his own deluded choice. This must go on until by God's grace the Divine Teacher awakens in him the purifying love for God which destroys his egoism and sets him free from all illusion. Bodily death is common to all who take the body, but it cannot affect God's lovers, who dwell not in their ego but at the Feet of God, spending their lives in continuous memory of him and self-identification with his Will.

The pleasures of the world for a time distract the seeking soul from its agelong quest and prevent it from the passionate search within, which would unveil the Hidden One in each heart. So

all-absorbing are these worldly delights, worthless though they
be, that they leave the soul no time to think of its own needs;
the senses are so busy tasting them that they forget their very
function is really to set God on the throne within the soul. So
the soul forgets God, intoxicating herself with pleasures that
turn to misery.

All earthly things are doomed because they are transient and
fleeting. They will perish. All friendships and relationships last
but for a limited period, and when death calls, the soul must at
once leave them behind. All man's wit, wisdom, his bodily
charms and strength, his wealth and courtliness, his noble
ancestry, his lands and houses remain behind and pass into
other hands; the soul must enter the unseen as naked as it came
into the world at birth. Death is always at the doorstep for each
one of us and it becomes us to think how much of that precious
Name of God is really treasured in our hearts.

Man can break the mental trappings of the flesh and rise to
communion with the Eternal within his soul. Family and
friends can be helpers and inspirers, when one seeks their parti-
cipation in the divine quest. But when he abandons himself to
their earthly cravings, they are manacles chaining his feet to a
low type of life. The world is transitory but life is immortal.
Man's physical existence is mortal but his Spirit is immortal.
Life may move from suffering to wisdom and peace or it may
fall from the pinnacle of sensuous pleasures into the pit of
sorrow and death.

Fear of Death and Fear of God

'The first duty of man is that of subduing fear,' says Thomas
Carlyle. 'We must get rid of fear, we cannot act at all till then.'
The fear of death is the greatest fear. Whoever acquires calm
fearlessness in the face of death attains godliness. The eminent
Sufi Dho-L-Nun Al Mesri sums up the situation thus:

Fear wasted me,
Yearning consumed me,
Love beguiled me,
God revived me.

And yet the Sikh scriptures stress the need of fear of God,
and clearly distinguish it from the other fears. It is this fear that

destroys all fear. This fear of God is in essence awe and reverence of God, and it has in it a moral direction towards achieving dynamic powers of fearlessness that knows not any other fear. It is the Fear that dispels all fears:

Entertain in the heart the fear of the Lord;
Through the fear of the Lord, all other fears are conquered.
Of what merit is any fear
That leadeth not to fearlessness,
But to other and worse fears?
There is no other place of sanctuary, O Lord but Thyself;
Nothing can come to pass but what Thou ordainest;
What fear should we then have except the fear of the Lord?
All other fears are but phantoms
Of the mind, too much attached to worldly things.

Violence, worldly love, greed and pride
Are insatiate like a restless river.
Unless the fear of God is thy food and drink,
Unless the fear of God is thy whole sustenance,
Degradation and death are thy lot. (*Sacred Writings*)

Fear inspired by terror and lower cravings and passions is the anticipation of evil and pain as contrasted with love and hope which anticipates the good. Awe, on the other hand is the sense of wonder and humility inspired by the sublime or felt in the presence of mystery. Fear at the earthly and material level of sensuous desires leads to helplessness of reason and will, while the holy fear of God is the acquisition of insights and higher morality. Guru Tegh Bahadur identifies the fearless state with the highest spiritual state of divine illumination:

He who fears no one,
Nor strikes fear in anyone,
Consider my mind, Nanak says:
Such a man to be Enlightened Sage.

A clear direction is given by Guru Tegh Bahadur here. A Sikh should neither fear any human power nor strike any fear in any fellow man under any circumstances. The mind and soul of a man who lives like a coward under the oppressive authority of some ruthless ruler will degenerate into a submissive and crushed Spirit, incapable of clear thinking and acting according to the dictates of his conscience. To conquer fear is to conquer greed and death. But there is a type of fearlessness which is associated with brute force and cruelty. Men with a dead conscience also act fearlessly, but this apparent fearlessness springs from callous ruthlessness. But a God-fearing man is compassionate, conscious of his inward strength, courage, energy of purpose and is unshaken in his faith and conviction in Truth and Justice. He conquers the minds and hearts of others through compassion, charity, understanding and love. Such a man is illumined with divine knowledge, and is a philosopher, scholar and sage, in the true sense of the word.

Divine Reckoning and Judgment

Many people are not able to reconcile the belief in a good and righteous God with the facts of life as they see them. Why do the wicked prosper? Why is God silent in times of disaster? The ultimate plan of God is not revealed in the happenings of a few years. Men sometimes have to wait to know what the final outcome will be. Sometimes one evil destroys another evil. Truth ultimately triumphs and lives even if it has to pass through severe tests of suffering. Evil may prosper for some time but it is ultimately doomed. The just shall live in the protection and sanctuary of God.

God the Indwelling Spirit, whose light resides in every heart as the living conscience (*antarjami*) judges every soul after death, taking account of every human action, thought and feeling and desire and giving a judicious and righteous return for all. All sins meet their ultimate chastisement sometimes in this world but positively after death. Deeds of merit bear their fruit. There is absolutely perfect reckoning and reward of man's deeds: *Othe saco hī sac nibde*. There everything is judged in the light of ultimate Truth. There is no partiality and no favouritism. No matter how powerful a man is on earth, in the Presence of God the sinner finds no escape. The Deity who Judges is called Dharam Raja, Azrael, and the King of Righteousness and is conceived to be an Omniscient Power of God created by him to serve the ends of Justice, but he is not God. Guru Nanak in his well known composition Asa di Var says,

Abandoning himself to wanton pleasures,
Man is doomed to lie in dust;
When from his body his Spirit departs
He who becomes a great man of the world
With chains around his neck is led,
And for his transgressions, he is tried.
After death he faces the reckoning of his deeds,
From punishment of his sins he finds no escape,
No one then listens to his woeful cries,
The spiritually blind wastes his precious life.

A scholar who sins will not be spared,
An unlettered saint will not be ensnared,
The scholar as well as the unlettered man
Will be judged by his deeds in his Court,
The self-willed and the boastful ones
Will suffer agonising blows.

If a burglar breaks into a house
And offers stolen property to a Brahmin
As charity in the name of his ancestors,
Even in heaven it will be deemed
As nothing but stolen property
It will bring shame and curse on the thief's race.
Even the Brahmin who in greed,
Accepts stolen money as offering,
Would lose his very hands,
Such would be divine Justice.
(Guru Nanak: Asa di Var, 3:3; 12:5; 17)

Those who become great and powerful through exploitation, sin and social crimes will not go unpunished by God. Man-made laws helped them in their evil designs but the ultimate Justice of God will chastise them for their misdeeds. In the world they could escape by bribery and corrupt practices but in the Presence of God and on the day of reckoning there will be no escape. For every crime against humanity and for every sin committed, a just punishment is given by the Dispenser of Justice. Violence against God, against Nature and against humanity is severely punished. All the hateful species of panderers and seducers who call evil good and good evil, darkness light and light darkness, and who have prostituted the things of God for gold and silver and made his earth a den of thieves, are dragged to the flaming tortures of hell and punished. Scholars who are sinners are not favoured for their knowledge. Charity given out of wealth that is stolen or amassed from exploitation of the poor is not acceptable to God. It is not Charity, and God punishes those who suck the blood of others and acquire social and political positions.

The concept of a Just and Omnipotent God demands that God will ultimately judge the deeds of every man justly. The Sikh Gurus did not believe that the dead will remain in the grave till the end of the world. The day of reckoning comes to every man immediately after death, and judgement based on Truth will be pronounced on everyone. Everyone suffers for his own deeds. Crimes collectively committed may have the same punishment, but the day of punishment may still be different. No one suffers for the sins of his kith and kin. Post-mortem judgment means God's ultimate assertion of his sovereignty over his creatures. 'The King of Death shall chastise him who has not cast down his self-will.' But the King of Death is the friend and servant of those who have attained enlightenment through the Word. 'Those who have been liberated by his grace escape the punishment of their sins: the King of Death tears the scrolls of their evil deeds.'

Heaven and Hell

Hell and heaven are states of mind and not geographical localities in time and place. They are symbolically represented by joy and sorrow, bliss and agony, light and fire. There is no such thing in Sikhism as eternal damnation or an everlasting pit of fire created by a revengeful God. Hell is the corrective experience through lower lives in which the hardened core of the ego of wicked people suffers in a continuous cycle of births and deaths in lower animals. God has given complete freedom and moral choice to man to prefer hell to heaven and to prefer divine love to both hell and heaven.

Man does what he wills in this world,
But straight is the path ahead which he must tread;
When a sinner is driven naked to the pit of hell
He looks horrible in his shame,
One has to repent for his sins and misdeeds.
(Guru Nanak: Asa di Var)

Hell is pictured symbolically as an intense and agonising experience which proves ultimately the indestructible nature of personality. Sikh religion and mysticism rise to the heights of disinterestedness and are free from the fear of hell or craze for joy and paradise.

Rebirth and Transmigration

The fact that man suffers for his bad deeds or is rewarded for good ones, leads to the theory of Karma. In Sikhism, the law of Karma, according to which we reap what we sow, is not inexorable. The burden of our sins, the taint of all past Karma can be thrown off, by diving deeper into truth, by leading a pure and noble life and above all by the grace of God. Human life is an opportunity to rise to immortal heights or fall into the pit.

In Sikhism there are two distinct doctrines which come into the category of rebirth. When the soul passes from one human life to another, in its moral and spiritual progress, it goes on acquiring human births till it acquires *Nirvana*. Such a rebirth is called re-incarnation and is a blessing and gift of God. It means that God out of his infinite mercy has given us one more chance to fulfil an ultimate destiny, and the seeker of Truth cries out, when he is at his Door, 'For many lives I have been separated from Thee, O Beloved. This life is dedicated to Thee and Thy Love.' Every man can cut asunder the bonds of birth and death during human life and attain perfection. The hope is extended by the Sikh Gurus to the lowliest of the low, to every human being living on the planet, no matter what his status, colour of skin or nationality and race.

Rebirth in the descending order is a punishment and a curse. The soul passes from lower and lower moral life as human being to rebirth in animal life and suffers untold agonies. Like a beast of burden he carries the load of his sins without any opportunity to get out of his present predicament. This is transmigration (*avagavan*, literally coming and going).

Spiritual Rebirth and Death and Life

Says Guru Arjan, 'First accept death, give up all aspiration to lead a worldly life; be humble as dust of everyone's feet and then come to me to be my disciple.' 'If you wish to play the game of love with men,' says Guru Nanak, 'Come to the lane leading to my Faith with your head on the palm of your hand. While treading on this path be not afraid to sacrifice your head.'

This path is described as 'narrower than a hair's breadth and sharper than a sword's edge.' A Sikh is expected to walk on this path with the spirit of martyrdom.

> Dead to the world,
> A Sikh lives in the Spirit of the Guru.
> A man does not become a Sikh
> By merely paying lip service to him.
> A Sikh dispels all doubts and fears,
> And lives a life of deep patience and faith,
> Verily, he is a living martyr. (Bhai Gurdas)

'Blessed are the dead who die in the Lord' (Rev. 14:13). Rightly are they called the blessed dead, for they remain continually dead to themselves and immersed beyond their own nature in the gladdening unity of God. This death of blessedness has little to do with physical dissolution: it is the letting go, the laying down, one by one of all the desires that seek their gratification in separateness from him. One by one these shackles have to be broken, the attractions disowned, and the illusions swept away. To die in the Spirit of the Guru is also to be called to die in the spirit of the Word of God, because the Word of God is the Ultimate Teacher. Guru Amar Das says, '*Shabad marai soi jan sijhai.*' He who dies in the Word attains the fruit of realization. Without the Word none can be saved.

Immortality and the Vision of God

In his strivings after perfection and in his efforts to dispose himself for the flooding in of mystical graces, the soul of the Sikh passes through a number of mystical states and moral conditions. Through moral and spiritual purification the soul journeys from one state of illumination to a still higher one until he reaches the Unitive State. Each state (*atmik avastha*) is the end of a past and beginning of a new future. A Sikh mystic leaves rapture and ecstasy far behind to reach the goal which is identification of the human will with divine Will. In this state God is there in the soul and the soul is in God. The five stages through which it passes are called: (1) the region of divine righteousness; (2) the region of divine illumination; (3) the region of Spiritual Beauty and Modesty; (4) the region of Grace; (5) the region of Truth and Light of God. The Cobbler Saint Ravidas describes the last realm as follows:

Realm of no-woes is the name of the city,
There is no sorrow or grief in that place;
There is no vexing harassment of taxgatherers,
There is no fear or sense of sin,
Nor is there any terror or deceit.
I have now acquired a beautiful homeland,
There is everlasting peace and goodness my friend.

The sovereignty of divine Spirit ever prevails here.
There is no second, nor third, only the One Eternal is here.
The City is ever so well known.
There the spiritually rich and affluent reside,
Who are prosperous and live in the richness of divine
Wisdom.

With full freedom they wander here where they
    of the inner apartment of the divine Palace
Do not obstruct or hinder their movements,
Says Ravidas, the liberated Cobbler,
He who becomes a citizen of my homeland,
Wins my esteem as my honoured friend.

(Ravidas p 345)

This is how man conquers death through the discipline of Sikhism, and becomes liberated. He thus achieves immortality while he is yet in mortal frame. Through Truth he visualizes Truth and lives with Truth. 'Thus the Lord's Elect (*Panc*) are accepted and embraced in his Presence. The pain of birth and fear of death is broken. They have attained the Imperishable Lord. Great honour is theirs in all regions.' And so the soul rises, climbing the five steps of the ladder of spiritual effort to his real home. By the faithful and brave execution of his duty on earth he earns the right to knowledge and wisdom, and so is enabled to make happy efforts in the helping of others. By this means he wins the grace of the Guru and so is led by him to union with the Beloved whom he has sought so long as the Ultimate Truth.

Death Ceremony

INTRODUCTION

(a) At the death-bed of a Sikh, the relations and friends console themselves and the departing soul by reading Sukhmani, the Psalm of Peace.

(b) When death occurs, no loud lamentations are allowed. Instead, the Sikhs exclaim *Wahiguru, Wahiguru!* (Wonderful Lord!).

(c) All dead bodies, whether those of children or grown-up people, are cremated. Where cremation is not possible, it is permissible to throw the dead body into the sea or a river.

(d) The dead body is washed and clothed (complete with all the five symbols) before it is taken out on a bier to the cremation-ground. The procession starts after a prayer and sings suitable hymns on the way. At the cremation-ground the body is placed on the pyre and the nearest relations light the fire. When the fire is fully ablaze, someone reads Sohila and offers prayers for the benefit of the dead. Then the people come away, and leave the relations of the dead at their door, where they are thanked and dismissed.

The bereaved family, for the comfort of their own souls as well as for the peace of the departed, start a reading of the Holy Book which may be at their own house or at a neighbouring gurdwara. Friends and relations take part in it, and after ten days they again come together when the reading is finished. The usual prayer is offered and Karah Parshad distributed.

(e) The charred bones of the dead together with the ashes are taken from the cremation-ground and thrown into the nearest river.

(f) It is forbidden to erect monuments over the remains of the dead, although monuments in their honour at any other place would be quite permissible.[1]

[1] Sections (a) to (f) from *Sikhism, Its Ideals and Institutions*, Principal Teja Singh, pp. 109–110.

The following hymns are usually recited during the funeral procession:

SOHI RAVIDAS

The dawn of a new day
Is the herald of a sunset,
Earth is not thy permanent home.
Life is like a shadow on the wall.
All thy friends have departed,
Thou too must go.
Thou believeth as if life
Were everlasting and endless,
The journey may be long,
Death is ever hovering over us.
Why art thou asleep?
Wake up, O simpleton.

He who gave thee life,
Gives sustenance also,
He is the soul of creation,
He is the all feeder,
Relinquish me and mine and worship Him
Within thy heart in the morning
Repeat His Name.
The night is on thee,
With its garments of gloom,
Life is coming to an end.
Thy feet have not found the path,
Says Ravi Das, Thou senseless fool,
Why dost thou not see,
This world is but the abode of mortal beings?

Know this O! Dear friend,
Clearly in thy mind,
The world is absorbed
In pursuit of pleasure,
No one cares for another.
Many wait in attendance,
Surrounding thee from all sides,
When fortune smiles,
When misfortune darkens the door,
They suddenly disappear and leave thee alone.
Even a wife who is loved and is loving,

As soon as the soul wings its flight,
Cries out, thou art dead.
Such is the way of them all,
Says Nanak, at the end,
God alone can befriend thee.

Mother, father, brother and son,
And the mistress of the house,
They cling to the living,
Soon as the breath leaves the body,
They leave it as dead.
Beware of the glamour of mirage,
Take heed and repent.
Says Nanak, repeat the Name of God,
Salvation is His gift.

Wake up, my mind, wake up,
From the dead sleep.
The body that came with thee,
Will part company with thee soon.
The world is but a dream.
Soon as life leaves the body,
Mother, father, and other relatives,
Will offer it to the fire,
They are only concerned with the self.
Says Nanak, sing the praise of God.

I found all worldly attachments false,
Every one is attached for the sake of his own pleasure,
Whether it is wife or a friend
Mine, mine, they all say, and cheat the heart
With expressions of love;
At the last moment not one comes near.
This is the strange way of the world!
The foolish mind does not listen
To wise advice and understand;
Says Nanak, he alone can cross the sea of being
Who sings the songs of God.[2]

[2] From *Sikh Ceremonies*, Sir Jogandra Singh, 1968 edition, Religious
Book Society, Chandigarh, India.

EDITOR'S POSTSCRIPT

We often hear about education for life, though this is too frequently limited in meaning to education for earning a living. Only rarely do we hear of education for death, though some educationists have held that, in view of the universality of death and the fact that we meet it in some form at every stage of our lives, this should be a primary, if not *the* primary, objective of all education. Such a view is at least a healthy correction to the prevalent tendency in contemporary society to avoid the mention of death and all its manifestations. The idea that children are unaware of death and need to be safeguarded from any contact with it or knowledge about it, is exploded in Dr. Brian Gates' chapter on Children Understanding Death. It emerges quite clearly from his investigations that they need to be helped to come to terms with it at an early age. I well remember a small boy of seven, who had lost his mother when he was five, looking at a dead tree and saying with a sigh 'everything dies.'

Concerning the meaning of death and what may lie beyond it, we have no knowledge, only faith; and for this reason some would regard death as an unsuitable subject for the classroom. Yet to avoid altogether a phenomenon we know to be universal throughout nature would hardly seem to be a sound educational policy. Nor would it be wise to ignore the beliefs and hopes which faith has kept alive in man from time immemorial. We may take the view that these are primitive reactions to an unfriendly world based largely upon ignorance, and the product of 'wish-fulfilment.' Yet psychological insight into 'primitive' myths arising from the unconscious and into archetypal representations of human experience since primeval time must give pause to those who would write off what is 'primitive' as unworthy of careful study.

In the contributions from different faiths in this book, and in the liturgical extracts, we have a summary of man's deepest faith responses to the world in which he lives and dies. Knowledge of these may be at least as valuable in helping us to come to

124

terms with the major problems of living and dying as any knowledge which is scientifically based.

There is another aspect of these contributions which we cannot ignore. If religious communities, previously somewhat isolated from each other, are now being brought into closer contact in pluralist societies throughout the world, certain qualities are required of religious people if they are to live together peacefully. With the Middle East and Northern Ireland in mind few would fail to recognise that the cultivation of those qualities has now become an urgent necessity. What are they? They have to do with awareness of and respect for the beliefs and social practices of others, with an openness of mind which, though not uncritical, is ready to learn from others and to welcome the new insights which learning brings, and with a readiness to welcome change and growth in spite of the pain which inevitably accompanies them.

The child who is being taught in such a way as to imply that there is only one viewpoint from which the truth can be seen is certainly not being prepared to live creatively in a pluralist society.

This book is therefore offered to teachers in the hope that they may use it to introduce their students to beliefs and customs different from their own and that in so doing they may help to prepare them for the adventure of living in the multi-faith society of which they are already members.